I0101425

The Middle Class Feeds Upon Itself

Chinese Mushrooms and American Jobs

Andy Leonard

THE MIDDLE CLASS FEEDS UPON ITSELF

ISBN:

ISBN-13: 978-0615998367

ISBN-10: 0615998364

THE MIDDLE CLASS FEEDS UPON ITSELF

DEDICATION

This book is dedicated to the Middle Class. To all of us that spend our lives striving to achieve the American dream. A dream that can be realized regardless of our self destructive actions. A dream that can be realized despite the actions of our politicians, both liberal and conservative, who selfishly pander to us for political gain. It is also dedicated to many of the 2% of Americans that provide many of us with jobs, investment opportunities and inspire us to achieve the dream.

THE MIDDLE CLASS FEEDS UPON ITSELF

CONTENTS

THE MIDDLE CLASS FEEDS UPON ITSELF

ACKNOWLEDGMENTS

Thanks to Nicole Bentley at A-1 Editing Service for her help with editing and Joe Tellep for the cover design.

Chinese mushrooms

There is a small can of mushrooms on my desk—Walmart's Value Brand, a paperweight in what has become a paperless world. The can label is marked "Product of China." I bought it at our local Walmart in Englewood, Florida. Why I call it "our Walmart" is beyond me, but I live with it. I lived in Allentown, Pennsylvania, and I can still visualize the Campbell Soup trucks on the highway taking American mushrooms grown in the area to their soup factory. Why aren't American mushrooms in these cans at Walmart? The answer is simple: price trumps "Made in America" and American jobs.

These Chinese mushrooms and all of the other foreign goods offered by American retailers highlight the decline of our ability, loyalty, or motivation to provide the basic blue collar jobs that were the underpinning of a once-robust American economy—not just a can of mushrooms, but a symbol of lost jobs in America. There was another can of mushrooms at Walmart next to the ones from China, which is produced in America. It was the same size as the ones from China and sold for three cents more per can.

The two cans say a lot about Walmart but even more about America. Looking at the facings—the amount of product facing the shopper on the shelf—it appears that for a lousy three-cents difference, most Americans are buying the Chinese mushrooms without a thought about the consequences, and would bet that they don't even know the difference between the two cans. They put their trust in Walmart's Value Brand and I'm fairly certain that because of the facings, Walmart makes a higher margin of profit on the Chinese mushrooms, even at the lower price. If only they could add another piece of information to the list on the back of the can, along with number of servings—about two—,it would be "number of American jobs lost!"

This isn't really so much to do about China. It is more about Walmart and the rest of the job killers like Amazon, Apple, Citibank, and other mega institutions—both public and private—that have become too big to succeed when American workers are taken into account. In their search for growth and dominance, they lose touch with, and disenfranchise, the American worker. It isn't just the recently-heralded great middle class or the traditional working class, but each and every American who gets paid for working, whether tending a drive-in window in Texas, waiting on tables in a diner in New Jersey, working on an assembly line in Michigan, or managing a high-tech development company in Silicon Valley. All are members of the upper class, middle class, lower class, and dependent class.

How many lost American jobs, both past and future, does my can of mushrooms symbolize? Millions! So how do you connect the loss of millions of American jobs with a small can of mushrooms? To me, that can is just a symbol of failure, a symbol not unlike the Apple logo, the Statue of Liberty, the Mercedes hood ornament, the Republican elephant, and the Democrat donkey. Most of us relate to symbols based on our individual frames of reference. If you're a Democrat, the elephant is bad. If a Republican, the elephant is good. The Apple logo is good if you're a

THE MIDDLE CLASS FEEDS UPON ITSELF

Mac user but not so good if you love Windows. The Mercedes hood ornament symbolizes the epitome of performance and quality, but a BMW owner might think differently. Americans cherish the Statue of Liberty as a symbol of freedom, but to our enemies, it symbolizes something entirely different. Each of us has personal and unique mental connections with various and sundry objects. I use the can of mushrooms to conjure up my experiences in the workaday world and my frustration with our current dismal job situation.

In order to understand our predicament, you have to connect the job dots in the workday world. Our politicians, the talking heads on television, and the parade of political has-beens—as well as the supposedly knowledgeable journalists on CNBC, CNN, and FOX—continuously talk about jobs but never mention specifics. Most of them are clueless and just don't understand either job creation or the infrastructure of jobs.

So the $0.75 can of Walmart Value Brand mushrooms sits on my desk and raises my blood pressure. I get so incensed that I'm thinking of substituting some other topping on my pizza—and I love sausage and mushroom pizza. It would reduce my frustration and certainly make me happier if my favorite pizza place would certify that their mushrooms are American grown. On second thought, I guess that you don't grow mushrooms—they just appear out of piles of manure. Fancy that! If this were how jobs were created, our politicians would give us an endless supply of jobs!

I started writing this as a form of therapy to both lower my blood pressure and as an antidote to the poison being spread by those clueless politicians and the parade of nitwits on the cable news channels regarding jobs. Don't ask me why, but I took the mushrooms from my desk and put them in the pantry. I distinctly remember telling my wife not to use them— she denies it. The short story is that I went to get them the other day, only to find that the Walmart mushrooms were gone. The love of my life had given the can to the local community food drive, but at least she kept the Giorgio American mushrooms.

She didn't understand the big fuss I was making over her blatant disregard for my attachment to the mushrooms. Her solution was for me to go get another just like the other one—she's my cheerleader. So I went back to the local Walmart Supercenter to pick up another can of Chinese mushrooms, along with some golf tees and an ironing board. The mushrooms had been moved to the bottom shelf, but there they were in the small white cans.

I bent down and picked one up and grabbed another, just in case the love of my life got the urge to make mushroom gravy. Grr! I looked at the back of the can to find the "PRODUCT OF CHINA" information, but it was gone. Instead of being happy that Walmart had seen the error of its ways and was now buying American mushrooms instead of Chinese, I was a little upset. So I got down on my knees and reached deep in the back of the shelf, hoping that there were still some cans with the dreaded "PRODUCT OF CHINA" information. No luck—they were probably doing a good job of rotating their stock. My proof of Walmart's greed was slipping away.

A store clerk straightening out shelves asked me if something was wrong. Evidently, their employees were well trained and on the lookout for old people in distress, and I was on my knees looking kind of sick. So I got up, thanked her for her concern, assured her that I was fine, smiled, and brushed off my knees as I got to my feet.

She went back to her duties as I began looking for some Chinese mushrooms and finally found them. My confidence in Walmart's greed was again reinforced when I picked up a 4.5-oz. jar of Walmart's Value Brand sliced mushrooms with "PRODUCT OF CHINA" on the back of the label priced at $1.25, next to a 4.5-oz. jar of Giorgio's Pennsylvania Dutchman sliced mushrooms at $1.36. The Giorgio jar had a little yellow outline of the United States with "AMERICA'S FAVORITE MUSHROOM' printed in the outline. Happily, I checked out and drove home, feeling better.

I didn't want to let my wife off the hook too easily though, so I thanked her again for donating my can of mushrooms to the hungry, informed her of the fact that there were no longer cans of Chinese mushrooms at Walmart, and asked her to go to the food bank and get mine back. *So solly*—fat chance! I then told her about the jars of mushrooms and the happy ending to my trip to Walmart. She looked a little relieved until she looked at the jars and gave me a twisted smile. *So solly* again! The jars of Pennsylvania Dutchman "AMERICA'S FAVORITE MUSHROOM" also had the dreaded "PRODUCT OF CHINA" on the back of the label!

In my mind, that made things even worse for Walmart. To me, it seemed like an insult to Walmart shoppers that by all measures, the most expensive jar by 9%—except for the label seemingly touting an America product—was the identical item as their Value Brand. Naturally predisposed to hold Walmart in low esteem, I felt my blood pressure rising again. They had the best of both worlds. If you bought on price, you reached for the Value Brand Chinese mushrooms. If you equated Pennsylvania with quality American mushrooms, you picked "AMERICA'S FAVORITE MUSHROOM"—also Chinese mushrooms. *So solly,* American jobs! You may think that this mushroom stuff is trivial, but it isn't. Most people, when thinking about American manufacturing jobs, look at automobiles, televisions, and other consumer goods. Mushrooms are nothing more than fungus, but fungus can kill you.

As a footnote to the mushroom saga, I found another can of Walmart's Value Brand Chinese mushrooms in a Walmart store in Cleveland, Ohio, on a recent trip back to my hometown. I deduced that mushrooms don't sell that well in Cleveland, or that Walmart perhaps changes suppliers frequently, or that the Cleveland store just doesn't rotate its stock regularly. To add to my frustration, I stopped in a Kroger supermarket in Atlanta on my way back home to Florida. They had mushrooms from India and Indonesia.

Do you remember the 1960s advertising jingle " Good things from the garden, garden in the valley, valley of the jolly , ho, ho ho Green Giant?" I always thought the garden in the valley was somewhere in Minnesota where they have that huge statue of the jolly giant. I am sad to say that the valley may have been relocated. I could be wrong, but I spotted a can of Green Giant mushrooms in the local Walmart and you guessed it—Chinese mushrooms.   Go figure!

2 Job Infrastructure

Before we can solve our jobs problem, we have to understand how we created this dilemma, which is an understanding of how jobs are created and destroyed. There is a reason we have a hard time creating jobs in this country. Politicians and bureaucrats are far too removed from the daily life of the average American. They, and the pundits and talking heads on television purporting to be experts on everything, are a long way from understanding the worker who packs a lunch, takes the kids to daycare or to school, and drives to his or her workplace.

Being retired, I watch and listen to a lot of the cable news these days from Fox (fair and almost balanced) to MSNBC (lean left), right thinkers to left thinkers. They're either the champions of big business and small government or the champions of big government and the little guy. To be sure, most of them parrot the current mantra of "it's jobs, jobs, jobs" but seem to have little understanding of job infrastructure.

Most of them are looking at the big picture rather than at the details of how jobs are created and how to sustain them over the long run. They all mouth the word "jobs," but other than "infrastructure jobs" or "high-paying green and tech jobs," they have no idea of what the average American perceives as a job. One thing is certain—government can create jobs, but most of them put a burden on taxpayers. It is insanity to suggest that in light of our current out-of-control government spending, we need to start tax-funded infrastructure projects that put more stress on the system. It' is a noble cause to rebuild our nation's ageing infrastructure, but how do we pay for it if there aren't enough working stiffs paying taxes? What good are new or rebuilt highways and bridges if the average American can't afford the gas to take advantage of them? What if he or she has no job to drive to on them? New roads to nowhere.

A favorite spot of mine on cable television is watching one of the left-leaning frenetic female talking heads standing in front of a dam and proclaiming that it takes a country to undertake such massive tasks and that corporate America will not. No doubt she's right, but it takes millions of taxpayers to fund these projects and in order to do so, they have to have jobs—private sector jobs. It is like putting the cart before the horse, or "I'll gladly pay you tomorrow for a dam you give me today."

Sure, the big projects create work, but only temporarily. A concentration of employees in a government-paid-for project in an area does create ancillary jobs. However, once completed, most of the jobs are gone, but unfortunately, the tax burden lasts forever. It is a top-down rather than a bottom-up solution and it just doesn't work over time. In order to build our first road or dam, our forefathers had to have up-front financing rather than a murky promise of future prosperity.

We're adding federal government jobs at an alarming rate while facing declining tax revenues and there's very little comment from our elected representatives in Congress. Evidently, the solution to the real unemployment rate—which is over 12.5% (U6 rate)—is to put as many people as possible on the federal government payroll. Instead of "of the people, by the people, and for the people, it is now "of the government . . ."

Current reports indicate that corporations are sitting on a pile of cash in the trillions of dollars and are refusing to invest it to create jobs. Companies in the Standard and Poor's Stock Index 500 alone have over 1.2 trillion dollars in cash. The consensus is that there's uncertainty on the part of business regarding government regulations that may come in the future. Companies also need cash in order to prepare for future downturns, but these concerns can't be the whole story.

Unlike government, a corporation doesn't create a job without justification—there has to be a need for it. There must be increased demand for its products or services, development of new products or services, or expansion into other businesses and markets. In our current stagnant business climate, it is no wonder that corporations are sitting on cash and if they finally decide to put it to work, it probably will be sent to other countries.

Are jobs created by small businesses or big businesses? The national debate goes on. I'm not sure that I agree with the consensus that the bulk of American jobs is created by small businesses. The answer is, it is both. It all depends on where you look and also on the definition of big businesses. In some parts of the country, a company that employs fifty people is big business, but in areas like Chicago and Pittsburgh, a company with fifty employees may not be considered big vis-à-vis the major employers in the area.

There are small towns and cities across America where one or more large business, industry, or organization dominates the economic picture. Just by their size and number of employees, they create hundreds of support and service jobs in the area, but when a key business or organization in one of these areas dies, it devastates the local economy.

Sometimes it is the county seat in a rural area. Farmers, ranchers, and local governments are what typically made county-seat towns prosperous with small restaurants, retailers, and service providers concentrated around the grain elevator, farm supply store, county courthouse, and government buildings. Many had a national retailer like Sears or Western Auto if the population was adequate to support them. The local grain elevator, feed store, and courthouse are still destinations in some areas, but county-seat towns, except those in populous areas, have been losing their attraction for quite a while. Mega-chains like Walmart and others decided which ones would survive.

In places like Kohler, Wisconsin, where the maker of bathroom and kitchen fixtures dominates the economy, there is a halo or multiplier effect. The city prospers because of the ancillary jobs Kohler creates. Kohler Industries, according to their website, have about 3,000 associates (or what used to be called "employees"). They have expanded into furniture and tile and they own two world-class resorts. In my mind, they are a job multiplier in America, even though much of their workforce is out of the country. What we need to create more jobs are more Kohler industries. It is a true example of the trickle-down effect on the local economy.

Historically, and on a much larger scale, are

THE MIDDLE CLASS FEEDS UPON ITSELF

Chicago, Illinois; Akron, Ohio; and Pittsburgh, Pennsylvania. Although much diminished, these American cities still are industrial and manufacturing centers with large local companies that, in addition to considerable workforces, spin off the ancillary support and service jobs. Most of our economic hub cities like New York, Chicago, Los Angeles, Philadelphia, Boston, Las Vegas, San Francisco, and Houston are a conglomeration of giant, large, and small businesses. How much of a multiplier effect from Wall Street does New York City get? It is incalculable, of course. The same can be said for Las Vegas with regard to casinos, or Houston from the oil business. Large businesses beget medium-size businesses that in turn beget small businesses. They keep airlines flying, hotels filled, taxis running, and an incredible array of service and support businesses flourishing.

The synergy of this conglomeration is awesome. It is also an incubator for individual entrepreneurs, from delivery services, decorators, and cleaners to hotdog vendors and taxi drivers. When businesses close down in these areas, the effects take longer to surface. There are millions of jobs in New York City. The impact of ten, or even twenty, lost businesses is hard to measure. It isn't like Kohler, Wisconsin. If Kohler Industries goes out of business, Kohler, Wisconsin, won't survive as it is. The wounds take longer to affect the job picture in these large cities but eventually, they take their toll and end up adding to the unemployment rolls. As the workforce in these areas shrink, the service-and-support businesses either contract or fall victims of what could be called a reverse multiplier effect.

The fixation with the idea that many new jobs are created by small businesses is misleading. It highlights the fact that there aren't many opportunities or reasons for big business to create more jobs. But for small businesses to start and prosper, we need fairly large-sized businesses—or conglomerations of them—that will be enablers for both medium and small-sized businesses. Again, big companies beget medium companies and both enable the small businesses to create jobs.

Infrastructure, infrastructure, infrastructure. Ask any politician about our infrastructure, and he or she will rattle on ad nauseum about building roads, bridges, and high-speed trains that create temporary jobs and that certainly will require taxpayers, who are employed long term, to fund. What they need to do is focus on our job infrastructure, but I don't think they understand it. How could they since few have any experience in the practical business arena? Most of them are career politicians and attorneys who have never had to start a business, meet a payroll of any size, balance a budget, or hire or fire an employee. They are a legion of lawyers.

The talk, or rather the static concerning new jobs, focuses on the illusory new high-paying tech or green jobs. The grim reality is that we cannot fill the black jobs in the oil industry in the western United States while Washington, DC, is creating jobs by the thousands that are being filled. Others say that jobs are not filled because the jobs are in one location and the qualified prospects are elsewhere. Such a situation is almost impossible to solve, as most Americans will not uproot their families and move to distant locations unless they are in dire straits or have the certainty or the promise of a job. It is often easier to stay put and collect unemployment insurance while searching for work, or waiting for something that pays better than unemployment to come along.

Unfortunately, in many cases, nothing does and we end up with a large number of the long-term unemployed, and it is hard to maintain skills and contacts if you're out of the workforce. Those who follow unemployment statistics often report that actual unemployment percentages are higher by two or three percentage points than the numbers stated in the monthly jobs report, and they represent those who have given up and quit looking. This is why the U6 rate is important as it represents total unemployment, including those who have given up looking for a job. Also, no one talks about the dramatic rise in the number of Americans on disabilities who aren't counted as unemployed.

Unemployment insurance has just about become limitless due to our legion of Washington lawyers. We're now providing unemployment benefits—for more than a year to some—without prudent funding. When was the last time your insurance company called you and said, "We're doubling your benefits and keeping your premium payment the same?" Or better yet, "doubling your benefits and getting the government—insert us—to pay your premiums?" There' is little or no motivation to take a job that pays the minimum wage while getting an unemployment check, particularly when you add the costs associated with maintaining a job such as food, fuel, daycare, and clothing.

The situation creates an increased dependency on government handouts. Why would someone on unemployment take a minimum-wage job? Instead of focusing on creating jobs for the unemployed, our legion of lawyers took the low road and attempted to renew the Emergency Unemployment Compensation again in early 2014.

One of the MSNBC pundits was talking about a new auto plant in the southeast. He pooh- poohed the fact that the $16.00 an hour jobs were lower-middle-class jobs and not what we need. Guess what? More than likely, all of the jobs would be filled with people who are blind to his self-serving-class label. I guess his idea would be for them to wait for one of those illusory upper-middle-class, high-paying tech jobs.

I wish our President would take the time to get in front of the American people and explain exactly what he means when he says we have to educate our children for the new green and tech jobs of the future. Is there some great innovative life change as we know it looming in the distance? I can remember, early in the computer age, when every large- and medium-sized company had to have its own computer department. There were millions of jobs created overnight including programmers, operators, field engineers, and system analysts. IBM was dominant and most companies created systems tailored to their business. The President's high-tech job speech would have been appropriate in the early seventies, but I don't think it washes today. Most new high-tech jobs are low-tech job killers and we may be better off without them.

What we really need is to reinvigorate our manufacturing capabilities. We need to start making the things we use every day in America again from toothpicks to tractors. Walk into any one of our too-big-to-succeed retailers and see what appear to be acres of the stuff we use every day. We used to make all of it here, but in our quest for lowest prices, we outsourced the manufacturing jobs and created huge

THE MIDDLE CLASS FEEDS UPON ITSELF

unemployment in the process. Recently, a factoid on TV stated that we have lost 4.000,000 manufacturing plants since 2000. We need to get them back! Those jobs, regained by the millions, would in turn create support jobs in sales, warehousing, services, and other areas. If someone on unemployment who had a $12-an-hour job could get one for $16 an hour, the impact on the employment picture might make the $12-an-hour job available again.

To someone working for minimum wage, a $15.00-per-hour job is high paying. If we could create enough $15.00-per-hour jobs, they in turn would generate higher paying jobs. A $15.00-per-hour job is about $30,000 per year. Four workers making $30,000 per year are far better for the local economy than one worker making $120,000 per year. Depending on their situation, the results could be four cars, four homes or apartments, appliances and furniture, plus other stimulants to the local economies like day care, restaurants, and entertainment.

The minimum wage is being discussed in our country, particularly regarding fast food and retail workers. Some say that the current $7.25 minimum wage should be raised anywhere from $10.00-$12.00 per hour. There have been sporadic protests and a call for a general strike by fast food and Walmart workers across the country. Raising the minimum wage is one of those feel-good things that liberals/progressives love to support. Evidently, adding $3.00-$5.00 per hour to millions is a sad comment on where we are if raising the minimum wage is one of the solutions to our job crises. Some believe that raising minimum wage workers wages would have no consequence to the middle class. Don't bet on it! By the way, if liberals re-branded themselves as progressive, we conservatives would be wise to start calling ourselves responsible.

Any responsible person understands that fast-food and retail businesses have always provided entry-level jobs into the general workplace. No one expected to support a family on these entry-level jobs. Most were part time and seldom lasted for more than a few years. I worked at an ice rink in Cleveland for minimum wage but never expected it to ever become a permanent job. High school and college students filled these jobs before they started a real job. Underlying the minimum wage issue is that the real jobs are gone by the millions, resulting in entry-level jobs being filled by older workers, some with families, with nowhere else to go. It is interesting to see the unions targeting these once-ignored workers and organizing some of the protests for a higher minimum wage.

MSNBC Morning Joe regular panelist Harold Ford Jr. made some comments regarding the minimum wage. To paraphrase, he indicated that we should find a way to pay older employees in a job a higher minimum wage than younger workers such as high-school or college students. Does that make any sense at all? Of course, it is a politician's unworkable solution to the problem created by the lack of real jobs available for the older worker. I think that there probably is a government subsidy (insert we pay) hidden somewhere in his solution.

To believe that raising the minimum wage to $10.00 per hour will create jobs and have no effect on the middle class is laughable. Prices will certainly go up. Who are Walmart's and McDonald's customers? Could it be the middle class? When the smaller local retailers, restaurants, and other businesses that are left to feel the impact, who will suffer? Could it be the middle class? It will certainly drive more business to the Internet and middle-class local business owners and employees will suffer. The big companies will use technology to reduce workers while smaller companies will become less competitive. The middle class feeds upon itself.

What upward pressure will raising the minimum wage to $10.00 per hour have on workers earning less than $10.00 per hour, but more than $7.25? What will the entry-level auto worker making $15.00 per hour expect? Of course, raising the minimum wage will have an upward ripple effect on all wages. The middle and dependent classes will pay the bill. You can be sure that the so-called progressives will blame it on the rich.

The pressure to raise the minimum wage is the dangerous result of America's inability to provide the real jobs that used to move people out of the entry-level jobs into better paying jobs. Certainly, the entry-level jobs are real but until recently, very few of us expected them to provide a living wage to families. We're in serious trouble. It is scary that our President went to the University of Michigan to give a speech touting raising the minimum wage to $10.10 per hour. He was backed by a cheering crowd. Most of the youngsters cheered the President, but I wonder if they weren't looking forward to getting a better paycheck after they graduate into one of those entry level minimum wage jobs.

Total student debt is approximately one trillion dollars. We're spending billions of dollars each year without regard for the consequences of an emerging workforce throwing up their graduation hats, only to find that the list of jobs that they feel qualified for is getting shorter and shorter. Before we can provide them with $40,000 to $60,000 per year jobs, we need to have a lot of $20,000 to $30,000 jobs. We may soon have large numbers of the most educated and underemployed college graduates.

There are over fifteen million college students in the United States. Many of them have substantial student loans. Where, and doing what, will they be able to find a job for which they believe they're qualified? Or will they be underemployed, taking jobs away from less educated but qualified workers? How many college graduates are working as servers in restaurants, security guards, or sales clerks in retail establishments because they can't find a job within their field of studies and are burdened with staggering debt? Too many of them end up back with their parents, thus postponing their independence.

This debt, which many of them shouldn't have incurred in the first place, will stifle their economic growth for a long time. One of our erstwhile legislators has proposed that if they have a record of ten years of faithful payments, their debt up to $40,000.00 should be forgiven (I wonder if my mortgage holder will give me the same deal). It goes to show you how out of touch with reality our leaders have become, groping for any solution to the problem and not focusing on the real one—jobs.

If we could put our high-school graduates to work in large numbers at $16--an-hour jobs, the medium- and high-paying jobs will follow. We need to fix the underlying problems with our job infrastructure in order to spur real job creation in this country. Unfortunately, few of our politicians understand the

THE MIDDLE CLASS FEEDS UPON ITSELF

multiplier effect that low- to medium-paying jobs have on our economy. One of our southwest Florida cities is promoting tourism with the message that for every forty-five tourists to Florida, one new job is created. If this is true, then how many jobs do forty-five workers making $16.00 an hour create?

When I worked in the Allentown, Pennsylvania area, we employed 250 workers in our distribution center. Very few of them were high-paying jobs, but we never had a problem filling them. Our employees came from throughout the area and their take-home pay was distributed to local governments and businesses. By some standards, we weren't a large business, but we had a pretty significant impact on the local economy. It' is hard to calculate, but the $6 million in payroll was substantial. We're sending our kids off to college to become doctors, lawyers, and engineers. Without a large population of warehouse workers, factory workers, mechanics, and other such middle-class jobs, who will support the lawyers, doctors, and engineers besides the government?

The middle class can probably be stratified by compensation. Using the $16.00-per-hour mentioned by one of the CNBC regulars as lower middle class as the bottom, and the $120.00 per hour ($250,000 per year) as the top, that is most of us—the millions of us that our leaders pander to with speeches and promises but for whom they have no action plan. Our President and legislators, regardless of party, can't get in front of a microphone without mentioning the middle class and promote the fact that they are the champions of that large but undefined group. The truth is that most of them are out of touch with, and simply don't understand, the problems that need to be solved in order to put the middle class back to work.

Andy Leonard

Talk is easy and cheap, and this is what we are getting from our so-called leaders. They all pander to the middle class. We need action and we need solutions, both of which are not coming from our President or Congress—all of whom have dismal but deserved ratings by Americans. Our re-elected President has promised to put America back to work. I hope he does, but I doubt his ability to do so.

3 To Big to Succeed in America

The long-term effects of allowing organizations and entities to grow uncontrolled have been devastating. They aren't too big to fail. They really are, for our own good, too big to succeed. We have been told repeatedly that some institutions are just too big to fail. Presently, because of our lack of financial regulations or the lack of enforcement thereof, this might be true, but for our economic health and jobs, we would probably all be better off without them. Mega banks, mega insurers, mega investment houses, mega retailers, and other mega corporations and institutions control too much of our economic life. Did I mention our mega government? We have bargained away control of our economic well-being for convenience, low prices, and supposed choice, and have lost many jobs in the process. And, of course, there is the mega Internet, one of the biggest job killers in history.

We have traded locally-owned-and-operated businesses for national conglomerates, so when a Home Depot opens in Florida causing local businesses to close, and a policeman in Illinois and a truck driver in Ohio get laid off because companies that supplied the local businesses were in their communities, who's to blame? We are. We have sold our economic soul to the national company stores such as Walmart, Home Depot, CVS, Citibank, Amazon, and others. We bypass local retailers for price. We order books, drugs, flowers, and movies without leaving our computers.

We charge them on a Citibank or Capital One card, bypassing local banks, and UPS or FedEx delivers them. Except for a small portion of our expenditure for the warehouseman and the person driving the truck, our dollars bypass the local economy.

It is estimated that every dollar spent locally travels five to eight times before it leaves the local economy. For every dollar spent at a local business, $0.45 is reinvested locally. For every dollar spent with the national chain, $0.13 is reinvested locally, and I really doubt that number. The national debate over jobs has taken a backseat to healthcare. We need to refocus on jobs, recognizing that our appetite for low-priced goods and services has resulted in millions of local jobs lost throughout our workforce. While pointing fingers at Mitt Romney and others of his ilk, the great middle class is feeding upon itself and outsourcing its jobs to other countries.

The growth of giants like Walmart, Amazon, Google, HP, Microsoft, and Apple not only eliminates jobs and competition, but their virtual monopolies impact our standard of living through wage depression in ancillary industries and professions, consolidation, demand destruction, and reductions in local, state, and federal services due to the lost tax revenue. The jobs destroyed by the growth of these massive brick-and-mortar retailers, technology companies, and Internet behemoths are unprecedented, except during the Great Depression.

The job destruction has caused a major impact on our local economies, an intolerable level of unemployment, heightened anxiety, a weakened housing market, and a fear of the future by many Americans. These establishments have become

THE MIDDLE CLASS FEEDS UPON ITSELF

economic thugs, preying upon the American workers and exploiting those in other countries while profiting from the American's middle class's penchant for the cheapest, latest, and greatest products and services. On the surface, low prices and convenience seem great for the public, but by allowing companies to get "too big to succeed," the hurdle for competitors to get in the game becomes too high, which has an unintended but devastating impact on the American economy.

Take a look, beyond the obvious impact, the huge retailers have on their competitors. Examine the job losses in the ancillary private and government sectors affected by—but not usually associated with—their growth. Smaller competitors close, wages fall, along with corresponding taxes, local newspaper advertising declines, and small businesses such as printers and accounting firms close their doors. As the government proposes tax-incentive schemes to create jobs, we ignore the root cause of pervasive job destruction by companies that have grown too-big-to-succeed in America.

To illustrate the impact of such companies on jobs, take any "commodity retail item" that you can find in a Walmart or Home Depot store. An example would be a Stanley tape rule or a box knife. Prior to the predatory pricing and purchasing practices by too-big-to-succeed retail giants, Stanley Works and other manufacturing companies made all or most of these products using American labor. In cities like New Britain, Connecticut, Stanley made the tape rule in many models from homeowner's use to contractor grade. The same can be said of the Stanley Knife or box cutter. On a trip to Home Depot today, you'll still see hundreds of Stanley items lined up on the hooks, including many tape rules and knives. As far as tools go, Stanley is an iconic American brand to many of us. A close look at the back of the product information cards will show that most of them are made out of the country now, but the Fat Max tape rule is one made in the USA. Stanley looks more like an importer than an American manufacturer. To survive the pressure from the too-big-to-succeed retailers, Stanley is now a predator, buying other companies, consolidating businesses, and eliminating jobs in the process. The local Home Depot has a large selection of Stanley tools, with the vast majority of them made somewhere other than in the United States.

Take a stroll down the Walmart aisles and you'll find merchandise from all over the world. In the clothing section, you will find the iconic American label Puritan (iconic to those of us over fifty) on clothing made almost exclusively in places like Sri Lanka, Singapore, and Bangladesh. Again, the country of origin is on the back of the tags. It doesn't matter what department, and I guarantee you that you will find that most of the merchandise—the stuff we used to make in America from toothpicks to tractor is "*hecho en* someplace else." And it isn't just Walmart! This past weekend, while shopping at a local but regional department store, I found the once-great Van Huesen brand on shirts made in South Africa!

We're destroying the job infrastructure that results from prospering local medium-to-large manufacturing companies. Too often, we look at buying imported products for a low price as a loss of only manufacturing jobs, but what about the American jobs lost in the supply chain that used to get these goods from American manufacturers to the retail shelves? Gone are the sales people and their support office employees who processed the orders, warehousemen that filled the orders, the truck drivers, accountants, etc. Certainly, some of these jobs would have been lost to technology regardless of where the products were produced.

The impact of factory layoffs on local economies can be devastating. When a worker's wages are reduced to unemployment compensation, the amount of dollars exchanged for local goods and services like restaurants, banks, day care, newspapers, health care, etc. plummets. This reduced amount and velocity of money creates anxiety in the business sector, causing a general belt tightening, and if it continues to persist—more jobs lost—the housing market gets depressed and fewer tax dollars are available for services.

This scenario has been repeated in all sectors of our economy from manufacturing to the Internet. By allowing it to continue, we may have one of everything—all of them being too big for our own good. All manufactured goods may get here by boat. Walmart may be the only retailer open 24/7 for all our needs, both brick and mortar and on the Internet. Google may be the only search engine and Apple may be our only door to the Internet.

Bill Simon, CEO of Walmart USA, on a September 23, 2013 CNBC program, said that Walmart has added 600 stores without adding an additional distribution center. This shows the unmatched power of their logistics system. Walmart was conducting a manufacturer's conference In Orlando, Florida, with 500 American manufacturers and other major retailers participating to supposedly re-ignite Walmart's desire to use US manufactured products.

Mr. Simon indicated that Walmart is committed to

buying $10 billion worth of American manufactured products over the next ten years. It is a relative drop in the bucket compared to Walmart's $443 billion in annual sales. And when he uses Walmart's volume cannon on suppliers, it'll come to pass—unless, of course, the price isn't right.

These ugly results of entrepreneurial excellence began with someone asking questions like, "Can we get a nice tape rule and retail it for $3.99 and make a profit?" Of course, this person worked for one of the retail companies that are too-big-to-succeed and the answer was "yes" because a "no" would result in a loss of business to someone else. I don't believe a vendor can say no to a Walmart or Home Depot very often without suffering dire consequences. Unfortunately, in many cases the result is a made-in-the-USA label replaced by a made-somewhere-else label. The retailer increases its profit margin and American workers suffer!

McDonalds sells more food with fewer employees. Walmart sells more merchandise with fewer employees. Amazon ships more goods with fewer employees. Microsoft sells more software with fewer employees. America's flattening GDP statistics show that we're doing more with fewer people. If you can stomach it, visit the two websites below and view the dismal pictures of our country's economic statistics.

http://www.bls.gov/eag/eag.us.htm

http://www.usgovernmentspending.co m/us_gdp_history

Anyone can see that an increase in productivity— without an increase in goods produced or

THE MIDDLE CLASS FEEDS UPON ITSELF

corresponding job growth in new or existing industries—results in fewer jobs. This quest for productivity has swelled our unemployment rolls and put a grim imprint on the American psyche. Yes, yes, I know we now have Amazon, Travelocity, and Netflix. The only problem with that is that I can't find an Amazonian, Netflixian, or Travelocitian that helps our local economy. I don't know any Googlonians either. Sadly, I do know many Yahoos and a few Twits—most of them in government.

Gone are the local booksellers, travel agents, newspapers, radio stations, and video stores. Amazon, in a quest to corner the market on everything ordered on the Internet, is planning on delivering some merchandise to customers who are close to their distribution by what can only be described as mini-drones. If they do, I'm buying a pellet gun. Unfortunately, I can use the services from these too-big-to-succeed companies without talking to a single human being.

Our politicians, who are many times removed from the real American working stiff's experience, have no clue or the intestinal fortitude to bring us back to reasonable levels of unemployment. Their solution is to promote large government infrastructure projects or to garner pork for their home districts, usually for short-term government jobs so that they can get re-elected. They wander the Capitol's halls in a fog looking for solutions to the job crisis. Solutions that have not been forthcoming. A legion of lawyers--God help us—can we still say that?

Too-big-to-succeed retail companies use their ability to sell large quantities of merchandise to beat up suppliers on price, packaging, and delivery. In many cases, this results in fewer choices for consumers. The retailer will offer exclusivity to a manufacturer in exchange for lower prices. Roaming through the tool section, Stanley Tools look pretty much like the exclusive hand tool supplier to Walmart. The same could be said of other products at Home Depot, and as the giants concentrate their business with one or two manufacturers in a product line such as tools, other tool manufacturers fade from the scene. There is both anecdotal and hard evidence everywhere.

This past holiday shopping season—I really mean the Christmas season—I was again roaming the aisles at our local home improvement center. There were massive displays of all kinds of handy tools and gadgets with contrived brand names with which I'm not familiar. When I was in the hardware business, it wasn't unusual for retailer to get a product from a manufacturer and put their private label on them. I'm sure they still do it. True Temper-made products for True Value with their True Test label on them. The reasoning is that the retailer gets a lower price and is responsible for the advertising instead of the manufacturer. In many cases, a label on the tool said "Manufactured by XYZ Company for True Value Hardware Stores."

Just about all of the products in the massive displays at my local Home Depot were made in China carrying brand names I have never heard of. It's my opinion that the reason most major retailers don't put their name on these brands is because they don't want to be seen as a supporter of foreign outsourcing of American jobs. I can remember one of the too-big-to-succeed retailers selling tools labeled "Ohio Forge," most of them made in China.

THE MIDDLE CLASS FEEDS UPON ITSELF

Price isn't the only thing the big boxes require from manufacturers that were pretty much forced by the retailer to have anti-theft devices, bar codes, and tamper-proof packaging. Gone are some of the jobs of pricing and restocking merchandise. In many cases, suppliers and distributors provide employees to stock shelves for retailers. If a manufacturer's merchandise doesn't conform to their standards and go smoothly through their supply channel, the supplier is punished by the loss of product shelf space and, in some cases, removed from entire lines at retail. The day-to-day interruption of supplies can result in the giant retailers fining the manufacturer thousands of dollars for loss of business. Cost cutting by too-big-to-succeed companies also has resulted in part-time workers comprising a large part of the retail labor force.

The too-big-to-succeed companies have become the darlings of consumers. Gone is Walmart's price-slashing smiley face and replaced by a simple slogan, "Save money. Live better." We need something better than MSNBC's powder puff piece on the giant but may be prevented by the fact that they are one of the biggest buyers of ad time. Who's to blame? We are! We all point our finger at someone else, but as from Pogo," We have met the enemy and he is us," the great American middle class. The broader but not-often-taken-view of the complex and interdependent support systems in the economy will demonstrate that the answer to Walmart's "Save money. Live better" may be "A better life without Walmart." The middle class is feeding upon itself.

Even though we seem to be in love with the many too-big-to-succeed companies, we also love to blame their greed for our predicament. The truth is that in our free enterprise system, it's the goal of all businesses to not only make just a profit but to maximize it. A lot of our personal wealth held in public and private retirement pensions, 401Ks, and IRAs can be attributed to the success of publicly-held companies as reflected in their stock prices. It's too easy to look to the large salaries and bonuses paid to executives of some companies and somehow use this as the reason we're losing jobs. Of course, many are overpaid, but there are few complaints when the Dow Jones Industrial Average tops 16,000 and pension funds and retirement accounts grow.

Home Depot, Apple, Walmart, eBay, Facebook, Pandora, and Amazon are the darling five-hundred-pound gorillas, but they're also economic thugs and large job killers in our local economies. The Internet and the ability to sell goods and services without having to open a door or ring up a register have spawned many of them. Many don't use the U.S. Postal Service, pay local taxes, advertise locally, or ever see hard currency.

Some would say that Internet companies do advertise locally. I get coupons via e-mail from many national retailers without any benefit to local businesses. The normal scenario is that a computer in Idaho takes an order from a customer in California, which is then shipped UPS from a warehouse in Arizona and paid via Pay Pal. We have accepted an Internet process that is efficient, impersonal, and job destructive. Thank you very much, Bill Gates or Al Gore.

The Internet commerce has hurt both local and chain store sales. Amazon, Netflix, and Apple certainly have caused many local businesses to close. Gone are the video rental and record and CD music retailers.

THE MIDDLE CLASS FEEDS UPON ITSELF

Major damage to local economies is really done by the on-line sales by the so-called brick-and-mortar companies. Walmart, Best Buy, and Staples reach out on the Internet to customers who're willing to pick up products at local outlets, often driving long distances to get them. This system puts up roadblocks to local entrepreneurial entries to the marketplace.

It could be that locally-owned, non-chain business is doomed as it's getting difficult for existing competition to stay in business. Locally-owned retailers such as hardware stores, drug stores, and tax preparers are finding it harder and harder to stay in business as shoppers order goods and services on the Internet. Sure, some of the local businesses are surviving the battle with the big boxes and Internet giants, but their numbers are dwindling and it's amazing that some stay in business.

Why would I, except to support a local business, wait a week or two for a softball glove from a local sporting goods store when I can visit twenty or more sites on the Internet, view two or three glove manufacturers' complete selection, and get it shipped today while paying less and avoiding a sales tax? And if I don't like it, I can send it back at no charge and get a replacement. Best Buy is now trying to combat the practice of consumers going to their retail stores to familiarize themselves with products and then ordering them online. Even a too-big-to-succeed retailer is being threatened by our love of technology.

In many cases, it's no longer the products but the delivery systems. Amazon, Walmart, Google, Microsoft, and the Internet itself have become such behemoths that they can add a product or service to their system and deliver it to the consumer with minor incremental costs and minimal labor expenditure. The bigger they are, the more efficient they become. Unfortunately, this isn't true of our government. This efficiency can and does crush competition through exclusiveness, predatory buying, and retail pricing. Walmart orders a shirt to its specifications from Sri Lanka, gets it on a retail rack in Kansas City nine thousand miles away for $6.99, and makes a profit doing it. Americans gripe when an oil company makes record profits but most have no idea of how much Walmart and other soft goods retailers make on goods imported from Third-World countries. Do we even care?

These giants have amazing power to eliminate competition and keep others from entering business. Walmart has become so large and powerful that they probably can lower prices in one city to drive local groceries, lumber yards, and specialty stores out of business. They can do it through a computer-controlled pricing scheme that allows them to tweak prices across the country by product, depending on competitors in the market. Once the competition is gone and they own the market, they can adjust the retail prices higher. A lower price in Chicago is offset by a higher price in Buffalo.

Amazon does it all. Go to their website and look at what they offer. What started out as an Internet bookseller now is a multinational Internet commerce company offering much of the stuff that we use, and a lot of it is *hecho en* someplace else. Many of the items that they sell go directly to the consumer from the supplier or from central warehouses strategically located to serve large geographic areas. They have not only taken out competitors and the thousands of jobs that would be supporting them, but they also have the benefit of tax-free sales in many cases. Local communities are losing out on millions of dollars due to the sales tax advantage that online retailers have been given.

Jeff Bezos has personally purchased The Washington Post for $250,000,000. I would suggest that Amazon's ability to sell goods without collecting sales tax and the consequent rise in its stock value helped make the purchase possible. You can't fault Mr. Bezos—he's doing his job, which is to maximize his company's profit.

On December 27, 2011, Sears and K-Mart announced that they would be closing one hundred stores across the country because of sluggish Christmas sales. Why? Without proof, I would suggest that the sales went to the too-big-to-succeed companies like Walmart and Amazon. At a conservative estimate of thirty employees per store, this amounts to three thousand jobs--just in the stores. What about the jobs in those companies that support the stores? What about the impact on jobs in the local communities, from the trash collectors to the local maintenance companies? How many of those store employees aided the closings with their Internet purchases? We are feeding upon ourselves.

There is this dilemma with technology. The more sophisticated it gets, the more jobs we lose. Look what has happened to the photo industry. It all started when you could send a roll of film to be developed and they sent you back your pictures and a floppy disk. Someone had to make the film, it had to be stored in a warehouse, shipped to retailers, sold to a consumer with a camera, returned to be developed, sent to a laboratory, sent back to the retailer, picked up by the consumer, and stored in a shoebox or photo album.

Today, you point your phone and in ten seconds, your 5,000 Facebook friends will receive the picture. No chemical manufacturers for the film, no film manufacturer, no shippers, no laboratories and no jobs. Of course, this is an oversimplification, but the process was quick and simple—five thousand pictures without the touch of a human being, except for the touch on the phone screen. Phone cameras are getting so good that soon, only the serious photographer will need a camera. Kodak, another iconic world manufacturer of photo products, has recently declared bankruptcy--didn't we all see it coming?

We're about to do the same thing with books. Before too long the book form of the printed word will be obsolete. Bookstores across the country are closing the same way that video stores and record shops closed. We've already done it with the encyclopedia, and who needs the Yellow Pages? A click on Amazon and a short download will get a book on your computer without the printer or the paper. This process will, of course, destroy jobs and will also destroy an author's enthusiasm for creative writing. Once a book is on electronic device, current or future technology will allow multiple copies to be spread across the Internet without the creator making a dime. So why did I make this an eBook?

Newspapers around the country are dying off, victims of the Internet. The same goes for magazines. Once labor-intensive, the publishing and printing businesses have vanished into the Ethernet. Local papers are disappearing, victims of reduced or non-existent local advertising and the vast array of information available on the Internet. Except for the great community information provided by our local paper, I would have no use for a newspaper.

Banks across the country are closing branches due to the growing use of on-line banking and banks operating only on the Internet. I would bet that most, if not all, of the jobs eliminated won't be those held by the dreaded 2% but will be middle-class jobs that are eliminated by the actions of the middle class. However, many will blame the 2%. The 2% grows richer, the dependent class expands and the middle class shrinks.

I guess the convenience justifies the end. It would be hard to argue that these job-killing technologies are bad for the public, were it not for the fact that they are erasing hands-on jobs by the thousands, if not millions. We're getting to the point where new technology jobs are destroying old technology jobs, and the result is increased productivity with fewer employees.

When the television replaced the radio as our prime form of entertainment, workers switched from one job to another. Unless we can bring back the manufacturing of techno gadgets like cell phones, game consoles, and computers, the result of new technology will be further American job losses in addition to the ones that have been lost to other countries. So our quest for low prices, convenience, and choice has created these too-large-to-succeed entities. I would argue that we should let them fail and reinvigorate our local economies.

An exception to this process has been our local, state and federal government. It is chilling that the biggest "too-big-to-succeed" entity that we all deal with is our government, local, state and federal. Not driven by the profit motive, they expand services until the till runs dry and the American taxpayer suffers the consequences. It was distressful to recently discover that the biggest new job market is in Washington, DC. We have ended up with elected elites. While other too-big-to-succeed organizations contract, consolidate, cut costs, and increase productivity, our government expands, strengthens bureaucratic power, pays no attention to costs, and is generally non-productive.

The day is coming when government employees and others that depend on taxpayer dollars for their livelihood—such as teachers, firemen, public transport employees and police—will comprise a majority of the voters in this country. Urban areas that are taxpayer money pits will have more and more influence on the political process. If private sectors jobs continue to shrink, there's little hope for the rest of us. It will be an unsustainable system where bureaucrats and public sector employees will dominate our political system and we will become Greece.

Another promo spot on MSNBC is Mr. Ed, from the show named after him, highlighting the attack on policemen, firemen, and teachers. I guess he equates the recent Wisconsin governor's fight with the state teachers as an anti-union effort. I didn't see it that way but rather, I saw it as a way to stop the unfair negotiations between teachers unions, and local governments. It is patently unfair to allow elected or politically-appointed persons to negotiate with one of the biggest voting blocs in an area. My experience with union negotiations is that it has always been in an adversarial environment. This usually isn't the case with teachers, firemen, and police.

A perfect solution for creating more jobs would be to somehow break up or limit the growth of powerful institutions, whether public or private. Amazon,

THE MIDDLE CLASS FEEDS UPON ITSELF

Google, Apple, Microsoft, and the major national retailers like Walmart, Home Depot, and Lowe's are job killers. The conundrum would be, are we willing to sacrifice lower prices and convenience for a healthy and robust local economy? Unfortunately, the answer is probably no.

And, fearing being labeled a Luddite, do something to reduce or eliminate commerce on the Internet. Millions of jobs would suddenly appear! God forbid that we would have to wait a week for something to be delivered to a local business. In addition to the huge sales tax advantage that Internet retailers have, they avoid the costs associated with having retail stores. Drive around most towns in America and you can see many vacant stores and empty space in local strip malls. Our phone and computer screens have replaced the stores and we the customer have replaced the retail employee. We feed upon ourselves.

Andy Leonard

4 The Disconnect of Wall Street From Main Street

A popular political talking point ballyhoos the apparent disconnect of Wall Street from Main Street. It's used typically to promote the idea that Wall Street's wages, ethics, and operations are out of control and need to be regulated and also, that Wall Street runs on greed and has no connection to the average American's economic plight. This may be true, but the real disconnect is in the jobs that are lost due to the too-big-to-succeed companies. Isn't the middle class's quest for the lowest price on everything the same as greed?

A review of the thirty companies making up the Dow Jones Industrial Average over the past fifty-plus years gives a view of great change. In 1959, the companies were predominantly manufacturers producing goods in America. Their success meant American jobs and prosperity. As stock prices went up, money was made and a lot of it was reinvested in America. Most of the Dow Industrial Index companies manufactured goods for American consumption and exported their products throughout the world.

The current makeup reflects a much different situation for American jobs. The companies now in the DJI Average are, to some extent, still manufacturing companies, but most of them are international companies with employees throughout the world. Many of them import products to America. No longer does their success mean prosperity for American workers. In fact, some of the tech companies and the two big retailers may be responsible for destroying countless American jobs in their pursuit of efficiency, lower costs, and bottom-line profits.

Apple Inc. has been on and off the most valuable company in America. I have an iPhone, my wife has an iPad, and friends have Apple computers. I wasn't surprised when I opened the boxes to find that the information sheet said, "designed in America and made in China." If someone thinks that "designed in America" will continue much longer, they must be drinking a special tea. Just like the manufacturing of these gadgets is predominantly somewhere else, the design jobs will go away. It makes me wonder if Steve Job's middle name was "Lost."

Back in the fifties and sixties, it was pretty much a guarantee that when the DJI rose, it meant prosperity for American workers and investors. Workers with pension funds administered by unions, governments, and private businesses had a direct connection to our prospering stock market. As 401(k)s and IRAs were introduced, more and more Americans were also connected. While American companies prospered, we expected that they would provide more jobs and prosperity for Americans.

There has been a gradual and ugly transition. Today is a different story. We have lost the jobs connection with many American companies. When the DJI rises, in many cases it means prosperity for workers in other countries. As a result, many American workers have been disconnected from Wall Street, both by lack of jobs and by the loss of the ability to invest through pensions and other retirement vehicles. If you had the money and wanted to invest in emerging economies, the Dow Jones Industrials is a good place to put your money. As the DJI rises, a lot of the jobs associated with it are in other countries. Some of the companies in the DJI are in the Standard and Poor's 100. A look at the NASDAQ, and you get the same results. As the companies prosper and stock prices go up, jobs are created elsewhere. And gone is Eastman Kodak.

The two retailers in the 2014 Dow Jones industrials, Walmart and Home Depot, show a stark contrast between the two retailers in the 1959 Dow Jones industrials, Sears Roebuck and Woolworth. In 1959, just about all the items sold at Sears and Woolworth were produced in the United States. Walmart and Home Depot rely heavily on foreign manufacturers for their goods.

The companies in the 1959 and 2014 DJI illustrate the enormous change in our economy. From being loaded with companies that provided American jobs, the DJI has transitioned to being dominated by companies that no longer rely predominantly on American workers. Here's a look at the changes in the companies making up the Dow Jones Industrial Average since 1959. Some would say that we have just transitioned to a world economy. You can't dispute that statement, but it's evident, looking at the list of companies, that the transition highlights the loss of millions of American jobs.

Andy Leonard

2014

3M	General Electric	Nike
American Express	Goldman Sachs	Pfizer
AT&T	Home Depot	Procter & Gamble
Boeing	Intel	Travelers
Caterpillar	IBM	United Health
Chevron	J.P. Morgan	United Technologies
Cisco Systems	Johnson & Johnson	Verizon
Coca-Cola	Merck and Company	VISA
Du Pont	McDonald's	Walmart
Exxon Mobile	Microsoft	Walt Disney

2011

3M	Du Pont	McDonald's
Alcoa Inc.	Exxon Mobil	Merck and Company
American Express	General Electric	Microsoft
AT&T	Hewlett-Packard	Pfizer
Bank of America	Home Depot	Procter & Gamble
Boeing	Intel	Travelers
Caterpillar	IBM	United Technologies

THE MIDDLE CLASS FEEDS UPON ITSELF

Chevron	Johnson & Johnson	Verizon Com
Cisco Systems	J.P. Morgan & Chase	Walmart
Coca-Cola	Kraft Foods	Walt Disney

1982

Allied Chemical	General Electric	Owens-
Illinois Alcoa	General Foods	Procter
	& Gamble	

American Can	GM Corp.	Sears
	Roebuck	

American Express	Goodyear	Standard Oil of
	CA	

AT&T	Inco	Texaco
	Inc.	

American Tobacco	IBM	Union
	Carbide	

Bethlehem Steel	International Harvester
	United Technologies

DuPont	International Paper Co.	US
	Steel	

Kodak	Merck and Company	Westinghouse
	Electric	

Exxon	3M
	Woolworth

1959

Allied Chemical	GE	Sears Roebuck and
	company	

Alcoa Inc.	General Foods CA	Standard Oil of
American Can	GM (NJ)	Standard Oil
AT&T Goodyear	Company	Swift &
American Tobacco	International Harvester Texaco	
Anaconda Cooper	International Nickel Union Carbide	
Bethlehem Steel	International Paper United Aircraft	
Chrysler Johns-Manville	Steel	US
Du Pont Owens-Illinois Glass	Westinghouse	
Eastman Kodak	Procter & Gamble Woolworth	

General Electric is a good example of the transition from American to foreign workers. In my working days at True Value Hardware, we sold billions of GE light bulbs and wiring devices. Many of the light bulbs were produced in Ohio. Walk through any retailers light bulb display today and you'll find rows of energy-efficient compact fluorescent light bulbs. They have the General Electric label on them and most or all are made in China.

THE MIDDLE CLASS FEEDS UPON ITSELF

Most would agree that GE represents one of the great and trusted "American Companies." Read the label on the bulb packages—they all contain mercury. Read the warning instructions regarding cleaning up the mercury if a light bulb is broken. We have had problems with toys, drywall, and other items from China. I don't have much faith in the safety of the bulbs from China and none in the Chinese government's monitoring of the production of these bulbs. Yet we're going to be required to use these bulbs in the future. Phillips Lighting—not a DJI stock— doesn't make its bulbs in China. Here are some of the EPA recommendations for cleaning up if one of these light bulbs breaks.

Have people and pets leave the room, and don't let anyone walk through the breakage area on their way out. Open a window and leave the room for 15 minutes or more. Shut off the central forced-air heating/air conditioning system, if you have one. Carefully scoop up glass fragments and powder using stiff paper or cardboard and place them in a glass jar with metal lid (such as a canning jar) or in a sealed plastic bag. Use sticky tape, such as duct tape, to pick up any remaining small glass pieces and powder.

Wipe the area clean with damp paper towels or disposable wet wipes. Place towels in the glass jar or plastic bag. Do not use a vacuum or broom to clean up the broken bulb on hard surfaces.

Carefully pick up glass fragments and place them in a glass jar with metal lid (such as a canning jar) or in a sealed plastic bag. Use sticky tape, such as duct tape, to pick up any remaining

small glass fragments and powder.

If vacuuming is needed after all visible materials are removed, vacuum the area where the bulb was broken. Remove the vacuum bag (or empty and wipe the canister), and put the bag or vacuum debris in a sealed plastic bag.

If clothing or bedding materials come in direct contact with broken glass or mercury-containing powder from inside the bulb that may stick to the fabric, the clothing or bedding should be thrown away. Do not wash such clothing or bedding because mercury fragments in the clothing may contaminate the machine and/or pollute sewage.

You can, however, wash clothing or other materials that have been exposed to the mercury vapor from a broken CFL, such as the clothing you are wearing when you cleaned up the broken CFL, as long as that clothing has not come into direct contact with the materials from the broken bulb.

If shoes come into direct contact with broken glass or mercury-containing powder from the bulb, wipe them off with damp paper towels or disposable wet wipes. Place the towels or wipes in a glass jar or plastic bag for disposal. Immediately place all clean-up materials outdoors in a trash container or protected area for the next normal trash pickup.

Wash your hands after disposing of the jars or plastic bags containing clean-up materials.

Check with your local or state government

about disposal requirements in your specific area. Some states do not allow such trash disposal. Instead, they require that broken and unbroken mercury-containing bulbs be taken to a local recycling center.

The next several times you vacuum, shut off the central forced-air heating/air conditioning system and open a window before vacuuming. Keep the central heating/air conditioning system shut off and the window open for at least 15 minutes after vacuuming is completed.

I for one would be a lot more confident when buying these bulbs if they were made in America. On a trip to one of the mega retailers, I dropped one of those curly bulbs while I was putting it in a deposit container for old bulbs and it shattered. I was waiting for the environmental police to cuff me and take me away. Instead, an employee said she'd take care of it. She casually swept it up and put it in a waste container. No special procedures, no hazmat drill—so much for environmental safety.

An ugly comparison of what has happened to manufacturing in the United States is that from 1929 to 1933, we lost 31% of our manufacturing jobs and from 2000 to 2010, we lost 33%. From a peak in 1977 when 22 % of non-farm payrolls were in manufacturing, the number fell to less than 9 % in 2012—a loss of more than 7,500,000 jobs. The number is even uglier when you add the support jobs that are generated by a flourishing manufacturing sector.

How long can we continue down this road? As American companies do their job, which is to maximize profits and return value to shareholders, they'll continue to outsource labor, taking advantage of lower wages in other countries. Stock prices will go up, the number of American jobs will go down, and the number of Americans sharing in the prosperity will dwindle. Just look at what happened to Kodak. There may be a time when instead of complaining, we'll be happy to man the call centers for some of the companies that have outsourced their production to lower wage and less regulated countries.

In 2011, the Occupy-Wall-Street-Main St.-Oakland, and in every other city, protesters were getting headlines in every major paper. Supposedly, they were protesting the greed epitomized by the Wall Street fat cats. A recent government study pointed out that the income of the top 2% of Americans has risen at a much higher percentage rate than the rest of us. A major reason for this startling statistic is that fewer and fewer of us are participating in the stock market. Many companies that matched a portion of employee's contributions to 401(k) plans have either reduced the matching contributions or traded American workers for foreign workers. Many have eliminated full-time workers in favor of part-time or contract labor. Some of these companies are included in the Dow Jones Industrial Average.

It is no wonder that there is a current dissatisfaction with Wall Street, but it's misguided. After all, a publicly-held company's duty is to return value to shareholders. If you want to pay $0.75 for canned mushrooms from China, you can't blame Walmart. Either pay the $0.78 for the American brand or shut up. Either pay the $15.98 for a shirt made in America or shut up. Either work for wages that will make America manufacturers competitive or shut up. Sure, the income of the top 2% of Americans is growing disproportionately relative to the wages of the rest of Americans, but I have a hunch that they would rather make their money from the efforts of American workers than those from China, Bangladesh, Viet Nam, Siri Lanka, or India.

All I can say is walk down Main Street and ask yourself, "Why I am disconnected from Wall Street? Could it be that I am as much or more to blame than the 2% of the Americans who have taken advantage of the system, have understood it, and have used it to their advantage?" The 2% has always been there doing the smart thing and really shouldn't be blamed for our dilemma. The difference is that though they are still investing in so-called American companies, many of the workers in those companies are in other countries.

We are experiencing what I feel is a temporary increase in home sales. Prices are rising and the number of sales driven by low interest rates is increasing. These increases are based on what have been years of declining prices and sales. As home prices go up, so do taxes and, eventually, interest rates. Mortgages will be harder for many to afford. Without an improvement in the unemployment rate, the housing market will stall. All the news reports dwell on the premise that home and retail sales drive our economy, which simply isn't true. Jobs drive the economy. Sooner or later, we must address the problem of how do we put more Americans to work in decent-paying jobs.

In his 2014 State of the Union message, our President indicated he would focus on income inequality in America. I hope he does, but unfortunately, I believe he will focus on how to redistribute the wealth of the 2% rather than on raising the wealth of the rest of us. When retailers close stores, banks close branches, and small businesses fail, it isn't the 2% that suffers. Most of the job losses are to middle- or low-income wage earners. Replacing those jobs is the answer. If we don't, wage inequality will continue grow. Increasing the minimum wage and equal pay for women in the work force are not going to do anything for creating jobs in this country. If anything, they will destroy jobs.

Radio Shack is closing five hundred stores across the country. Probably someone in the 2% made the decision. The same probably holds true for closing bank branches. I would venture that the decisions were made due to the actions of the middle class. We shop online, bank online, and push carts loaded with foreign-made stuff through the checkout lines of our too-big-to-succeed retailers.

5 About the Mushrooms

Life is full of epiphanies, ordinary daily occurrences that create a leap of understanding. At sixty-nine, I've had my share. Witness the time in the sixties when I succumbed to an ad and bought a kit for building an AM/FM receiver. Halfway through the process, as I looked at a jumble of wires and bad solder joints, I realized that I was wasting my time. The same thing happened when I tried piano lessons. Both experiences saved me a lot of frustration and wasted time. Picking up a can of mushrooms in Walmart didn't change my life, but it clarified my understanding of our current dismal job picture.

Now retired, I keep pretty active in the most-of-the-time warm Gulf Coast of Florida. My wife and I have lived in Rotonda West—peculiar spelling—for the last eleven years. We are actually part of Englewood, which is south of Sarasota and north of Ft. Myers. It' is a quiet town with a great beach and has yet to be discovered by the baby boomers. We like to call it a fishing village with a drinking problem. It is near where the September 11th terrorists learned to fly airplanes into buildings and where Hurricane Charley hit in 2004. It has also been hit with Walmart, Home Depot, Walgreens, and CVS.

To be fair, I must confess that I love to hate Walmart. I worked for True Value Hardware, the national hardware store chain, for thirty-plus years and watched Walmart put many True Value stores out of business, sending their employees to the unemployment lines.

I avoided shopping the retail giant while working for True Value as it was like consorting with the enemy. Here in Englewood, as in most small towns, options are limited. We do have a True Value, Ace Hardware, and a few local stores that have adapted to the big box competition and focused their inventory mix and service to the area's needs, but I am still forced to shop at Walmart for a lot of stuff. So, grumbling, I walk their aisles checking labels and content descriptions and noting that very few of the items in the store are made in America—a fact that Americans have been complaining about for years—but still push cartloads of the stuff through the checkout lines. A lot of the folks pushing those carts once were staunch union members but now they have no compunction against shopping at a store that has always been anti-union and checking out using the self-checkout lane. So much for loyalty!

On a recent trip, I wandered into the grocery side of the store. I expected to see produce from other countries and did. I couldn't believe it when I picked up a can of Walmart's Value Brand Mushrooms and found that they were a product of China. How could that be? Pennsylvania is the mushroom capital of the world! I remember seeing a sign proclaiming this when I lived in Allentown. Campbell Soup trucks were ever present. Chinese canned mushrooms in Florida? What's up with that? And to add to my astonishment, at the end of the same shelf and occupying about one-tenth of the shelf space was the same-sized can of mushrooms that were products of Temple, Pennsylvania. The Chinese mushrooms were $0.75 and the Pennsylvania mushrooms were $0.78. They appeared to be the exact same product, but the

THE MIDDLE CLASS FEEDS UPON ITSELF

American mushrooms were 4% higher than the Chinese. What was the point of the American mushrooms? Were they sort of paying lip service to "Made in America" and catering to those shoppers seeking American products?

It is over seven thousand miles from Beijing, China to the Walmart store in Englewood, Florida. It can't be possible to get those mushrooms all the way from China at a cheaper retail price than from Pennsylvania—about one thousand miles distant. It isn't just impossible, it is just plain wrong. Someone at Walmart decided that we wouldn't mind and made a conscious decision to put their private label on Chinese mushrooms. And Americans are buying them because they are less expensive than American mushrooms and we live better because of Walmart, right? It all began to cave in on me. That can of mushrooms was an ugly reminder and a symbol of all the American jobs lost during what has become the Walmart era. And it isn't just the Walmart era. It is also the Home Depot, Lowe's, Apple, Target, Amazon, Netflix, and Google era.

It isn't a well-known fact that True Value is a co-operative — individual entrepreneurs who leverage their collective buying power to get the best prices from suppliers. This collection of local owners of stores across the country enables them to compete to some extent with larger retailers. Ace Hardware is the same type of organization and there are others in the hardware, drug, and grocery business.

The co-ops really thrived from the late 1950s through the mid-1980s. Many of these businesses and other retailers like the Western Auto and Ben Franklin stores helped make many small and mid-sized

American cities prosper. Members of retail co-ops were able to compete with big city retailers like Sears, JC Penney, and others. Of course, some called the co-ops communist.

The founder of True Value Hardware, John Cotter, was a workaholic. Although the storeowners were members of the co-op, it really wasn't a franchise and they were free to buy merchandise from any source. John constantly reminded the storeowners how important it was for them to concentrate their merchandise purchases through the co-op. It would maximize their buying power and thereby increase their ability to get the best prices from the manufacturers and compete with the big boys and franchise stores.

He ran a no-frills organization, which he called a bare-bones operation. Although he could drive any car that he wanted, a bare bones Chevrolet was always in his parking slot. His constant goading of the members and his stubborn hands-on managing style resulted in an amazing growth chart. He had a poster of the chart in his office with a quote from Walter Winchell under it that read, "Nothing recedes like success." True Value and many other small retailers prospered. A ripple in the retail waters that started with the owner of a Ben Franklin store in Newton, Arkansas, would become a killer wave that would wash many of them away.

Although it started in the early sixties and was incorporated in 1969, Walmart was pretty much an unknown to most retailers. The retail universe was centered in Chicago and New York City and Sears was the dominant player. While True Value and others were hammering manufacturers for the best price, Sears was using a gun. Sears merchandise managers,

THE MIDDLE CLASS FEEDS UPON ITSELF

because of Sears huge volume, could take up all of many manufacturers output and negotiate the lowest price possible. Well, if Sears used a gun, the rapidly growing Walmart organization would bring out the cannon.

I watched from the True Value distribution center in Kansas City, Missouri, where I was working as Walmart expanded in the region. With over 200 stores by 1980—mostly in rural areas of the middle southern states around Arkansas—I saw the wreckage. The expansion was like a blitzkrieg, devastating many small-town retailers and turning vibrant towns into dull patches of empty businesses and lost dreams. Many of the True Value stores were the first to be flattened by the Walmart tsunami. Prior to Walmart coming onto the scene, to lose or close a business because of a more aggressive competitor was common. An Ace replaced a True Value or a Western Auto was replaced by an OTASCO store, but it wasn't the same with Sam Walton's machine.

Opening stores in the county seat or other centralized towns, Walmart sucked in the retail sales from businesses in an expanding circle. Small retailers weren't just replaced; they just disappeared. The loss of the hardware, sporting goods, automotive supplies, drugs, clothing, and other retailers devastated many small towns. Their payroll and tax dollars and profits were the threads in the fabric that are essential for a small town to prosper. The local service and entertainment businesses were supported by these dollars. Newspapers and radio stations relied on their advertisements. Local governments survived on the various taxes collected. A lot of small town America went from happy times to dire straits in a relative instant.

Sure, the county seat towns enjoyed a short period of prosperity. New customers from the surrounding towns now came to their Walmart. They bought gas and groceries, ate at their restaurants, and patronized other service businesses, but it would be short lived. Walmart's aggressive retail steamroller soon included banking, hairdressers, eye care, gas, fast food, and other categories of goods. Local businesses either couldn't compete or had to settle for the retail dollars that fell through the cracks in Walmart's retail floor. Now, they advertise a phone plan and a drug plan along with a major health care provider. There are studies to the contrary, but it is pretty obvious that many, many jobs were lost in the process.

As long as I worked for True Value, my wife and I never, or almost never, shopped at Walmart. For every dollar we spent at Walmart, a few cents were used to eliminate some of our hardware stores. We supported local retailers whenever we could or bought at Walmart's dwindling national competitor list.

After retirement in 1995, I realized that the battle was lost. Walmart was now the only retailer in some areas. It dominated the American retail scene and became the largest retailer in the world. In our city in southwest Florida, Walmart is the epicenter. And to feed our craving for all things in big packages, there is a Sam's Club within a fifteen-minute drive from our home. Life is grand. I still try to give my retail dollars to the scant selection of local retail businesses when possible, but I now shop in the aisles of the behemoth while hating every minute of it. As I

THE MIDDLE CLASS FEEDS UPON ITSELF

said, I have long ago reluctantly conceded the retail war to the few giants and watched the diverse local retail scene steadily morph into what can be described as "Green Wall Depot." I can only hope that indeed "nothing recedes like success."

Some would say that we can never go back and that the jobs are lost forever. They could be right. A twenty-year-old entering the job market today was born in 1994. He or she has no frame of reference as to when most of the stuff we used was made in America. Just about all of the stuff they use, including cell phones, game consoles, computers, and clothes are *hecho en* someplace else. It would be crass to say they didn't care, but I don't think they give it much thought.

Not only have we surrendered the ability to make the stuff that we use every day but also our ability to grow what we eat. We have surrendered to countries that in many cases are thousands of miles away and to workers who have no idea what the products are used for. Entire layers of our job infrastructure have been surrendered. I believe Americans should realize that we are a cooperative. We should concentrate our economic activity for our collective benefit, whether we are in the top, middle, or bottom of the economic strata. If we do this, we'll prosper. We need to commit to America.

THE MIDDLE CLASS FEEDS UPON ITSELF

6 From Made in America to *Hecho en* Someplace Else

In 2003, China evidently became the largest producer of edible mushrooms in the world, making it the mushroom capital. And Walmart, arguably the most sophisticated logistics company in the world, either by choice or due to competitive retail conditions—if you can believe it—decided to put its private Value Brand label on the Chinese mushrooms. I could understand that for the can of mandarin oranges that also had the Walmart private label on it, but mushrooms? How does the largest company in America dare to insult the American farmer and worker by selling him Chinese mushrooms to put on his American-Italian pizza?

When I started working for True Value in the early 1960s, I worked on the receiving dock. It was just the opposite of the current situation. Almost everything that came into the warehouse was American made—Stanley tools, Corning Ware, Black & Decker, Rubbermaid, and hundreds of other American brands. The exceptions came in what we called rice-paper cardboard boxes and contained cheap items that were made in Japan. I remember the comments that could be sifted down to "who in their right mind would buy this kind of crap?" What a difference half a century makes. Now, 35% of the parts in the Boeing Dreamliner come from Japan and most of the products that we use every day are made someplace else.

Andy Leonard

Making stuff was what we did, from toothpicks to tractors. The jobs provided by American manufacturing were critical to the foundation supporting our economy. From janitors to CEOs, manufacturing jobs were everywhere. We rolled all of our steel, copper, aluminum, and other metals. Our mills, smelters, and foundries fed the system. Small machine shops made parts for local manufacturers that made bigger parts that fed production lines across the country.

The American garment industry was thriving. The output from the production lines and textile mills was the items that we used every day. Most of the pills that we take used to be produced in America. Today, no antibiotics are made in America. Where did these jobs go? We now rely upon China and India for all of our antibiotics. China produces most of the aspirin in the world. Think about it the next time you take a pill. More than likely, it comes from a place with a regulatory process that is much less stringent than required by our Food and Drug Administration. We used to make what we use, and that meant jobs—American jobs.

The high school that I attended had classes in foundry, machine shop, drafting, and other subjects to prepare students for manufacturing jobs in the Cleveland area. We had a Ford plant, a Chevy plant, and a Cadillac tank plant. Tool-and-die shops were everywhere. Some of the Southeast side's streets were orange tinged from the grit spewing from the steel mills. A high-school graduate could always find a job, and a good many of the jobs were in the manufacturing sector.

In Cleveland, we had Ridge Tool, another iconic American brand famous for their pipe-working tools and their calendar. Every gas station had a Rigid Tool calendar hanging on a wall somewhere—young boys made it a point to know where the calendars were displayed—usually out of sight from female customers. Viewing their website today reveals that they are still manufacturing in the USA, but also in Germany, Switzerland, and, of course, China (the calendar is available online.)

Except for some automobiles, consumer goods, and most of our food, we quit making the stuff we use every day. It started with those cheap items in rice paper boxes and the odd person who bought a VW Bug or another little foreign car. It happened while we were listening to the Beatles, launching space vehicles, and building computers and the Internet. The stuff we used every day that was made somewhere else began to be accepted.

The imported transistor radios, Honda Civics, and cheap calculators from Japan made a small dent in our GDP. The categories would grow and end up and include places like Sri Lanka, Bangladesh, India, and China. As the dent expanded to include more and more of what we used, Americans complained a bit about quality, but price trumped quality and we settled. After all, our cars were still the best and what harm could come from these cheap products? Not to worry—we still made most of the items we used every day. Walmart had its cute little Zorro and pirate smiley faces streaking across TV screens and slashing prices with a sword. Gone was the time when Walmart touted its "made in America" products.

We received over 24,000,000 twenty-foot shipping containers at American ports in 2010, most of them filled with items that used to be made here by

American manufacturers. There are around 12,000,000 unemployed in our country. You do the math.

Why have we lost so many manufacturing jobs? Eventually, the price pressure on manufacturers from too-big-to-succeed retailers caused them to use importers that outsource products to low-wage countries, thus killing American jobs. This process worked so well that the manufacturers gave more of their products to importers for manufacture, killing even more jobs. Soon, most of their products were imported. This process continued to the point that the retailer bypassed the manufacturer and began importing complete product lines. More manufacturing jobs were outsourced, followed by the much-ballyhooed customer support help desk jobs, but few complaints were heard because you never had to talk to the foreigner making the tool or shirt.

When companies like Stanley sold product to smaller chains like Sentry Hardware and others, they used factory representatives who called on the buyers at the chains. In some cases, a factory rep would represent multiple lines of merchandise to the chains. National account managers sold products to the large chains like Sears, Penny, OTASCO, and Montgomery Ward, working directly for the manufacturer. As these chains went out of business, the infrastructure of factory reps and their support staffs were pretty much eliminated, costing thousands of jobs. I don't believe anyone sends a factory representative to Walmart these days. More than likely, an executive of the company calls on them for sales. Walmart's current TV commercial touts the fact that they keep prices low by eliminating the middleman. It wouldn't sound the same if Walmart said that it keeps prices low by eliminating the middle jobs.

THE MIDDLE CLASS FEEDS UPON ITSELF

The following is a partial list of retailers that are either out of business or consolidated with others and that will give you a good picture of what has happened to both national and regional retailers as a result of the actions of too-big-to-succeed retailers and technology. The list is partial and unedited from Wikipedia with the following permission http://creativecommons.org/licenses/by-sa/3.0/. I urge you to go to this site http://en.wikipedia.org/wiki/List_of_defunct_retailers_of_the_United_States to see the devastation wreaked upon large and small cities alike by the too-big-to-succeed retailers like Wall Mart, Home Depot, Amazon, Walgreens and others.

Automotive

4-Day Tire Stores, 10,000 Auto Parts, Auto Palace, Auto Source, Auto Works, Big Wheel/Rossi Auto Parts, Checker Auto Parts, Chief Auto Parts, CSK Auto, Guarantee Auto Stores, Kragen Auto Parts, Murray's Discount Auto Stores, Nationwise Automotive, Oklahoma Tire & Supply Company, Parts America, Schucks Auto Supply, Super Shops, Trak Auto, Western Auto,Wheels Discount.

Camping, sports or athletic

Gart Sports, Galyan's Trading Company, G.I. Joe's, Herman's World of Sporting Goods, Mages

Oshman's, Olympic Sports, Sportmart, Sportswest, Sunny's Surplus

Catalog showrooms

Ardan, Best Products, Brand Names, Brendle's, Ellman's, Service Merchandise, H. J. Wilson Co.,

Witmark

Clothing, shoe and specialty stores

A&N Stores, Anderson-Little, Contempo Casuals, El Bee Shoes, Harold's/Harold Powell, Harry Levinson's, J. Brannam, Jay Jacobs, Judy's Inc., Just For Feet, Kids "R" Us, Kids Mart, Kinney Shoes, Kleinhans, Klopfenstein's, Laura Ashley, Martin + Osa, Merry-Go-Round, Raleigh's, Richman Brothers, Robert Hall, Rogers Peet, Roos/Atkins, Ruehl No.925, Sagebrush, The Sample, Sibley's Shoes, Thom McAn Store, Today's Man, Yellow Front Stores, Warner Brothers Studio Store, Petite Sophisticate, Mondi, Gadzooks.

Department and discount stores

Department stores involved with Federated and May

Many American department store chains and local department stores, some with long and proud histories, went out of business or lost their identities between 1990 and 2005 as the result of a complex series of corporate mergers and acquisitions that involved Federated Department Stores and The May Department Stores Company, and that resulted in many stores becoming units of Macy's, Inc. The following is a list of the affected stores, including some local and regional stores that earlier had been absorbed into chains that became part of Federated, May, or Macy's.

Abraham & Straus, Bamberger's, The Bon Marché, Bullock's, Bullocks Wilshire, Burdines, Carter Hawley Hale Stores, Davison's, Famous-Barr, Filene's, Filene's Basement, G. Fox & Co., Foley's, Halle Brothers Co,

THE MIDDLE CLASS FEEDS UPON ITSELF

Sanger-Harris, Gold Circle, Goldwater's, Goldsmith's, Hecht's, I. Magnin, Wanamaker's, The Jones Store, Jordan Marsh, Kaufmann's, L. S. Ayres, Lazarus, Liberty House, Marshall Field's, Meier & Frank, Co., Rich's, Robinsons-May, Stern's.

Other department stores

Alabama Duncan's, Dunnavant's, Gayfer's, Hammel's, Loveman's, Mazer's, Montgomery Fair, Parisian, Pizitz, Rogers. **Arizona** Babbit's, Bashford-Burmister, Broadway Southwest, Diamond's, Goldwater's, Jones & Hughes, Korrick's, Levy's, Sanguinetti's, Steinfeld's, White House, Yellow Front Stores. Arkansas MM Cohn. **California** A.G.E. , The Akron, The Broadway, Brock's, Breuner's, Buffum's, Bullock's, Butler Brothers, Carithers's, City of Paris Dry Goods Co., Daly's, Disco Department Stores, Fedco, FedMart, Fedway, Gemco, Gottschalks, Hale Brothers, A. Hamburger & Sons. Harris Department Store, Hart's Department Store, Henshey's, Hink's, Hinshaw's, Kahn's, Levee's, Liberty House, I. Magnin, Mervyns, O'Connor, Moffat & Co., Prager's, Rhodes, J.W. Robinson, Rosenberg's, Two Guys, Unimart, Steele, Faris, Walker Co, Weinstein's, Weinstock's, White Front, Whole Earth Access, **Colorado** Broadway Department Store, Crews - Beggs, The Denver Dry Goods Company, Gano-Downs, The Golden Eagle, Hibbard and Company, Joslins, A.T. Lewis, Neusteters, Perkins Shearer, Pueblo Store Co., Wellsworth Department Store., Fashion Bar. **Connecticut** Ames Department Stores Inc., Arlan's Department Store, Brown Thompson's,D&L (Davidson & Leventhal), D.W. Rogers Co., The Edw. Malley Co., E.J. Korvettes, Fairfield Store, G. Fox & Co., Grant's, Howland's Department Store, Howland Hughe's Company, Genung's Department Store, Kamen's, Luettgen's Ltd.,

Marlow's Department Store, Raphael's Department
Store, Read's Department Stores, Sage-Allen,
Seapark's Department Store, Shartenberg's
Department Store, Skydel's, **Delaware** Almart,
Bradleys, Braunsteins, Hoy`s $.5 and $.10, Nichols,
Strawbridge and Clothier, Wilmington Dry Goods,
District of Columbia Garfinckel's, Hecht's, Jelleff's, S.
Kann Sons Co., Lansburgh's, Palais Royal, Raleigh
Haberdasher,Woodward & Lothrop, **Florida** Burdines,
Cohen Brothers, Falk's, Furchgott's, Ivey's, JByrons,
Jefferson Stores, Jordan Marsh, J.M. Fields, Maas
Brothers, May-Cohen, Parisian, Richards, Robinsons of
Florida, Gayfers, Foxmoor. **Georgia** Adler's,
Chamberlin-Johnson-DuBose, Cofer Bros., Cullum's,
Davison's, Fine's, Goldstein's, Hogan's, J.B. White, J.
M. High Company, J.P. Allen, Jones, Kessler's, Kirven's,
Leon Frohsin's, Levy's, Michael Brothers, Muse's,
Regenstein's, Rich's, Saul's, Upton's, **Hawaii** Liberty
House, **Idaho** Blocks, Davids, Idaho Department Store, **Illinois**
Ackemann's, Block & Kuhl, Bressmer's, Community Discount, The
Fair, Goldblatt's, Lewis's, Linn & Scruggs, Henry C. Lytton & Co.,
Madigan's, MainStreet Chicago, Marshall Field's, Maurice L.
Rothschild's, Mayflower, McDade's, Montgomery Ward, Morris',
Myers Brothers, Robeson's, Shopper's World, Joseph Spiess
Company, Chas A. Stevens, Thrun's Department Store, Turn Style,
Venture Stores, Charles V. Weise Company, Wieboldt's, Zayre,

Again, to include the entire list would take up too
much time, effort, and space, so I included only the
partial list to illustrate the devastation. Go to the site
and see for yourself. Too casually, we refer to these
companies as brick-and-mortar retailers. They are
brick, mortar, and employee retailers. It was sad to
see that one of the defunct department store's
buildings in downtown Cleveland is now a casino.

I am familiar with the hardware retail business,

but the above is a good look at how many retailers are gone and with them, millions of jobs from janitors and receptionists to CEOs. Most had separate supply chains including sales reps, warehouse workers, truck drivers, and local retail stores. The wages these people earned traveled through local economies, providing jobs for millions of Americans.

The unintended job and tax revenue loss from business supporting these manufacturers and retailers is huge. Incalculable are the job losses from advertising and marketing companies such as graphic designers, printers, radio and television stations, outdoor sign producers, newspapers, and others. There are also the warehouse service companies like pallet rack and conveyor manufacturers, warehouse system designers, waste management companies, pallet manufacturers, propane and electric lift truck sales, propane and battery suppliers, warehouse designers and builders, and vending companies servicing employees, just to name some, and jobs in their support businesses like accountants, consultants, lawyers, restaurants, health providers, health insurers, pension administrators, union managers, airlines, car rentals, etc.

Manufacturers with American names like Milwaukee Tools, Levi, Buck Brothers, Irwin, Kohler, Wiss, Crescent, Rigid, and many others are either fully or partially offering foreign-made goods. Some of them display a patriotic symbol on the front of USA made products and a small print, "Made in China," on the back of other product packages. And not all of them are low-end products. It is sad yet almost comical when a package reads *hecho en* China instead of the expected *hecho en Mexico* or assembled with foreign materials? What does that mean? How in the world can we sell imported heavy toilets made in China for less than American made? Unfortunately, we may have accepted as a nation the fact that we can't make what we use and can't change *hecho en someplace else* to *hecho* in America.

These companies supplied jobs to all strata of job seekers, whether college or high school graduates or not. All of them are critical to a strong economy. If we are making appliances, tools, shirts, or answering customer support phones in America, those workers are buying other manufactured goods, new and used cars, homes, health insurance, computers, cell phones, gasoline, and groceries. They eat out, go to movies, and contribute to charity. They have savings accounts, pension plans, or retirement accounts. The money they spend is the lifeblood of our economy and eventually puts millions of Americans to work. Unfortunate parallel job-killing processes were occurring throughout our economy in companies that would prove to be too big to succeed.

The unfortunate fact is that we are content with the proposition that manufacturing jobs are being cut and replaced with so-called high-tech jobs. The problem is that the ratio of replacement jobs to lost jobs is terrible and results in unemployment in high numbers. What high-tech job is a guy who worked on an assembly line making some kind of widget capable of filling? Where is the janitor going who took out the trash, cleaned the lunchroom, and washed the windows? I don't think it's Amazon.com.

Counties are suffering, as jobs are lost across the country because of the declining manufacturing, retail and agricultural sectors. Young people leave the area to look for work leaving behind an older population. As

THE MIDDLE CLASS FEEDS UPON ITSELF

the population dies off, the counties contract or die completely.

Manufacturing, both heavy and light, supported many of these counties. So today, when the Wall Street reporters comment on retail sales, the only mention is of the-too-big-to-succeed companies like Walmart, Home Depot, Lowe's, and the Gap—retailers selling products that, for the most part, are made someplace else—but never mention the ghosts that are gone from the retail scene. And certainly, they give no mention the hundreds of thousands of employees who have vanished due to the consolidation in our retail and manufacturing base. Why don't we look at the jobs lost when government agencies approve corporate mergers? Financial reporters wring their hands because consumption is the driver of our economy rather than production.

We are content to walk the aisles, search the Internet looking for bargains on products that are made elsewhere, and ignore the workers who have shifted to the unemployment lines due to our quest for the lowest price. Sometimes you get what you deserve and reap what you sow!

Andy Leonard

7 Job Destruction

When the discussion turns to jobs in America, the focus is on job creation. There is not only a need for job construction in America but also a need for job destruction. The way I look at it, any time that you can eliminate or replace a government job, you eventually put money in the American taxpayer's pocket—this is good job destruction. In today's technology-driven society, private business has reduced employees, consolidated operations, and eliminated waste to increase profits. Government, on the other hand, increases employees, adds to the bureaucracy, and pays lip service to eliminating waste. Washington, DC is a mecca for job-seeking Americans. It has become a money pit for tax dollars and special-interest groups and lobbyists.

One of the unintended consequences of streamlining and computerizing our medical system into one giant database will be the loss of entry-level jobs across the country now performed by hundreds of thousands of middle-class clerks throughout the medical industry. It will be another paperless process utilizing scanners and cloud computing that will destroy American jobs. You can be sure that the government bureaucracy won't lose a job and will find a way to expand or replace these private-sector jobs, probably with higher-paying, public-sector administration jobs at the expense of a dwindling number of American taxpayers. Is that a good thing?

We have lost manufacturing, and low-tech jobs to

other countries. Some—and I would argue a low percentage of them—were replaced by new high-tech jobs. The problem is that many of the new advances in technology kill other tech jobs so we may have had an increase in tech jobs, but they were jobs that many are more than likely destined to be self-destructive. It isn't like Ford increasing sales at the expense of Chevrolet, resulting in a shift of workers from one company to the other—the shift is to the unemployment line. Give me a million low-tech jobs and I'll give you thousands of service and support jobs. We need to get back to the past and revive and retain jobs making products that we use every day.

Look at how technology and the Internet have destroyed jobs in the music industry. When cassette tapes replaced records, eight-track tapes replaced cassettes, and CDs replaced eight-track tapes, at least someone had to manufacturer something to put in a device to hear the music. The devices and media had to be made, shipped, warehoused, shipped again, and placed in a retail store. Today, billions of compositions are snatched—both legally and illegally—from thousands, if not millions, of places on the Internet. The proposition that the Internet would bring more royalties, more good artists, more good music, and more diversity to our music hasn't materialized. A recent sound bite on one of the cable shows explained that the majority of downloads is from old music. Whether true or not, I think that's a good thing.

Proponents argue that, were it not for funding public broadcasting, many Americans would be missing some great content. This sounds like a good argument, but why should their narrow audiences be funded with public money? With the exhausting variety of content on cable TV and its 24/7 news coverage, Internet

THE MIDDLE CLASS FEEDS UPON ITSELF

access to the same content, and every possible viewpoint on the news, what is the point?

Do we really need the McNeil/Lehrer news hour on the public nickel? With satellite radio you can get most of the same content, any genre of music, most worldwide sporting events, and political talk from both sides without national public radio. Look at C-SPAN? They seem to do a good job without government funding. During the past election, much was said about killing Big Bird, one of the most lucrative franchises in the country and the world. We don't need to finance any more Big Birds with tax dollars. Downton Abbey, the great PBS series, would have been a success on any network.

The same goes for the arts. We are supposed to believe that some artists and entertainers would be missed unless we use public money to nurture their talents. Again, this makes no sense. With all the outlets available for their work and talent, how could it be—if they are so talented—that they can't get recognition? Not to sound cynical, but it is more likely that if they had the talent, they could find a private outlet for their work. It is easier to use the pretense that their work would go unnoticed and unfunded to justify public financing.

Sequestration started a debate on government spending. Sure, public radio and television are very small government expenditures. Eliminating them wouldn't put much of a dent in the deficit, but if you were trimming the family budget, would you start with your mortgage or the $4.00 lattes? Public radio and television are the $4.00 lattes.

When it comes to government, job destruction is almost always good. When a publicly-held company

73

gets bloated with employees, fails to react to customer needs, or doesn't make an effort to contain costs, there is usually swift justice. It is economic accountability and is a self-correcting process. Prices go up, market share is lost, the stock price goes down, and eventually costs are either controlled or the company goes out of business. The painful self-correcting process is clearly evident in the recent upheaval in the American auto industry. The GM bailout was brutal and took much longer than necessary because of government intervention. In the end, they reduced wages, cut employees, dipped into the public till, and in the process, many GM retirees were severely hurt.

There is no self-correcting process in government. Our federal government is so big and so self-protective that there is no practical way to measure it, let alone manage it, and we all know the old axiom, "if you can't measure it, you can't manage it." If someone asked you, "Is the Environmental Protection Agency efficient?" how would you measure it? What about the Department of Homeland Security? I guess we all feel safer because of it, but at what cost and with how many unnecessary government jobs? Nobody knows the answers. The self-corrective process in the private sector is powered by the risk to employees' jobs resulting from poor performance. There is little risk in our bureaucracy for poor performance due to the fact that we can't measure outcomes.

Our local, state, and federal governments are proving to be too big to succeed. One thing for sure: the number of regulations per government worker cannot measure government efficiency. Complaints abound regarding our current Congress's lack of production. They have not passed the many new laws and the number of laws passed by Congress is a terrible measurement of quality. Just about every new bill or law restricts, hinders, or complicates life for someone. We should be thankful for the lack of production!

Better measurements should be used, like the amount of tax dollars collected per government worker or the cost of the average government worker. They would be good statistics for mayors, governors, and presidents to cite when giving their state of the city, state, and union speeches. It would be a start. We owe more than we take in, cannot control expenditures, and have too many government employees, and yet we refuse to face these facts. It is estimated that we spend $1.40 for every dollar that the government receives in taxes. If we choose to manage and solve our bloated government problems, it will be a long and painful process, but if we don't solve those problems, we will soon be Spain, Italy, or maybe Greece,

Andy Leonard

8 Class Warfare

Over this past election season, many politicians were engaged in a damaging, deliberate, and dangerous game of populist political pandering that was initiated and championed by our President. His constant reference to the middle class as a group that deserves tax breaks, stimulus money, and other government largesse plays well with many Americans. After all, if the middle class deserves it—to use a term not stated but implied by the President—the lower or dependent class voters deserve it too and the top 2% of Americans can get along on their own. Thank you very much! I can't recall ever hearing our President publicly giving any credence to the thought that the 2% have anything to do with job creation. I wonder if they can get a refund of all the money they contributed to his campaigns.

President Obama is quick to say that he is part of that 2% of Americans that earn more than $250,000 per year and is, for lack of a better but equally ugly term, the upper class. I have never heard him or other politicians use the terms "upper or lower classes." He insists that he and the rest of the upper class didn't need the extension of the Bush tax cuts because they already spend as much as they can and the billions saved by those taxpayers are desperately needed. Who needs these savings? You guessed it: the middle and dependent classes. Does this mean that the upper class will save the tax break money rather than spend it? Isn't that a dangerous proposition? At the end of

2012, he backpedaled and, in a political compromise with the Republicans, granted all of us middle-class voters a continuance of the tax breaks. So much for sticking to your guns, but he finally got the 2% and made the middle class happy. Really?

Pandering to all of us middle- and lower-class Americans is a calculated political move but one not very presidential. Our President got to keep the Bush tax cuts for all of us, but not for the upper class. The notion that some Americans should pay the way for other Americans is becoming an acceptable alternative to pulling yourself up by your bootstraps. Instead of one for all and all for one, it's "what's yours is mine," which seems to have been the driving idea behind the Occupy-Wall-Street mob, group, organization, gang, and/or political movement. I'm astounded to hear friends voice their opinion that if you can afford something more than I can—including taxes—you should pay more than I do. They never go so far as to say that they should pay more than the person who doesn't make as much as they do, but that must be what they mean, so what you really need is a graduated pay scale for everything.

I guess it means that if you go to a ballgame, your ticket prices should be based on income. Someone making $250,000 per year would pay $50 for a bleacher seat and the ball team would pay someone on unemployment $50 to sit behind the dugout. What an equalizer! We could also have a graduated sales tax based on income. I can see the gas stations now—forty prices for regular and only one for premium. Yes, the idea is absurd but just absurd as the notion of many Americans that someone else should pay for what they get. As is the current vogue, it is easy to apply the idea to taxes, but just let our legion of lawyers get their hands on such a system.

Our President used the issue of extending the Bush tax cuts to avoid addressing the unprecedented unemployment that has bogged down our economy and depressed the American psyche. He rallies the middle and lower class against the job creators. Doesn't he understand that across the country, doctors, restaurant owners, and other professionals and entrepreneurs create many jobs?

So let's do the numbers. There were approximately 126,832,000 voters in the 2012 presidential election. If 2% of them, or 2,537,000, were the 2% that our President continually rails against, then it makes sense to have pitted the other 124,295,000 voters against them. Our President received 65,899,660 votes to win re-election. Roughly 50,000,000 Americans are below the poverty line. I sometimes wonder if they voted to maintain the status quo.

Nationally, individual entrepreneurs have created millions of jobs over the years. The list is long and includes Bill Gates, Steve Jobs, Oprah Winfrey, Warren and Jimmy Buffett, Larry Page, Sergey Brin of Google, Pierre Omidyar of eBay, and Jeff Bezos of Amazon. Unfortunately in the long run, the growth and success of the companies in the tech industry the likes of these men created may have resulted in a huge net loss of jobs. In addition, according to *Forbes Magazine,* 339 large private American companies employ four million people. Within these millions, aren't there a lot of the upper-class villains? They include thousands of owners, officers, middle managers, and employees holding stock in their companies. They are the ones who do the investing and business expansions that result in non-government jobs. Just about all of our publicly-held companies were started by them.

The President insists that the rest of us will spend the money rather than save it. He believes that somehow, it's better for America if the middle and lower classes spend their continued tax windfall on flat-panel TVs, iPhones, Game Boys, and other stuff made in China. That is a spending extravagance that could possibly send some of the middle class to the lower class. Didn't excessive spending by all classes help get us into this mess in the first place?

President Obama avoids any reference to the possibility that the upper-class villains may put their continued tax windfall to use hiring some of us middle- and lower-class Americans. It's easy to understand his position. Although he is a self-proclaimed member of the upper class, his work history shows that he has never held a position where job creation was necessary. His work experience has been as a beneficiary of the wealth of the upper class and taxpayers' money. His advisory team is bereft of job creators. We have put a man in charge of our country most of us wouldn't trust to be in charge of our 401(k)s.

I have never been fortunate enough to get to that magical $250,000 income number, but my wife and I worked our butts off trying. We never considered ourselves middle or upper class. We were pursuing the American dream. The political pandering to the middle class has somehow made 2% of the population villains. Over the course of my working life, practically all of my jobs were for companies that were started by one of those upper-class villains. They worked long hours, took huge personal risk, and employed thousands of people. Now our President wants to punish them and in the process, he has—whether or not intentionally—diminished their contributions to our economy. It's easy to rally 98% of Americans against the top 2%, but what's the point other than to create class discontent?

Why our President wants to punish and alienate 2% of Americans is beyond me. His, and the populist rhetoric of others, is dangerous. They are bringing the concept of class warfare to the American dialogue. This isn't constructive and can be very destructive. Not a day goes by without some national politician pandering to the middle class, but of course that's where the votes are. Do our President and our legion of lawyers really believe that the American middle class is ignorant enough to fall for their rhetoric? From the results of the last election, it looks like it is. The constant bashing of millionaires and billionaires for the advancement of a liberal or socialist agenda portends future grief for our country.

This constant reference to classes is disheartening. What will happen when the middle class revolts against supporting the dependent class? Many Americans, some deserving and some not, put a huge tax burden on both the middle and upper class. Who gets Medicaid? Who pays for Medicaid? Who gets food stamps? Who provides the food stamps? For the most part, we are a benevolent society, but this may not be the case forever. The elected—and highly unpopular—governor of Florida signed the bill that would require welfare recipients to be tested for drugs in order to receive benefits. With very few exceptions, interviews of Floridian men and women on the street showed that they approved. Fear of the bill stopped thousands from taking the test. Of course, the ACLU

resisted it and a federal judge blocked its
implementation.

I'm sure that groups or individuals will rally
against this issue. Their hearts are probably in the
right place, but if there is widespread abuse of the
system, I don't believe that the average taxpayer will
sympathize with them. It may be an ominous sign that
Middle America, so loved by our President and
politicians, is not as tolerant as they would like it to be.

What happens when the middle class is fed up
with the drain put upon taxpayers by the dependent
class? Millions of Americans, in one way or another,
depend on taxpayers to provide them with food,
shelter, and other services. Eventually, Americans are
going to question whether their drain on the system is
legitimate. What will happen when the focus turns
from the abuse at the top 2% of Americans to the
bottom tier of Americans? Are they a bigger drain on
our economy than the said 2%? No one knows. Just
like drugs, it is just about impossible to measure the
cost of the dependent class on the rest of us. Because
of their large numbers and their ability to swing
elections, politicians avoid confronting the issue.

The sad fact is that the middle class is devouring
the middle class. We shop online; buy a lot of things
made in other countries, and keep in touch with each
other without talking to each other. We embrace
technology that is one of the biggest killers of
American jobs. The middle class rails at the top 2% of
Americans that just may provide jobs for them. The
middle class continues to send their kids to college but
has no idea as to what kind of jobs they are going to
have once they graduate.

Watching the talking heads on the endless cable

shows can make you ill. One survey shows that 70% of Americans believe we should increase the tax rate on wealthy Americans while 60% show that we shouldn't touch entitlements. Duh, of course they do! It is a "them, not me" attitude. In Florida, we take the same stance regarding real estate taxes. We tax non-residents, who own property but can't vote in Florida, at a different valuation structure than residents. We ignore the fact that they, for the most part, don't use our schools, spend much less times on our roads, and make few demands on our government services. When you discuss the issue, a frequent answer is that "if they can afford two homes, they can afford to pay more in taxes."

I don't know why I continue to raise my blood pressure watching the morning cable shows. They continue to fan the class warfare fires. They emphasize polls that highlight the fact that the vast majority of Americans favor increasing the taxes on the 2%. They never ask a question like, "Do you favor a serious crackdown on the excessive abuse by the dependent class?" It irked me when I heard MSNBC's Mika, the reincarnation of Lucile Ball and Gracie Allen, rail against one of the GOP primary hopefuls as he questions the motives of the "Occupy" folks. Most Americans that I know also question their motives but alas, most of these Americans are older and "occupied" places like Germany, Italy, Japan, Korea, and Viet Nam. Across the table from her is the same pundit who called the $16.00-per-hour jobs in the south "lower-middle-class jobs."

The nasty 2%, while the middle class has been devouring itself, is doing what they always have done. They have invested in the companies that have prospered by the actions and needs of the middle-class masses. The problem is that those companies have lost their economic connection to most of the middle class. While the 2% increases its wealth by buying stock in Walmart, Apple, Home Depot, Amazon, and the like, the politicians and pundits pit the middle class against them for succeeding in American capitalism. The middle and dependent classes, through their love of these too-big-to-succeed companies and entities, drive the stock prices up and put more money in the pockets of the 2% and then blame the 2% for investing wisely because of their actions.

The networks keep up the class dialogue with a steady stream of polls showing that the majority of Americans favor increasing taxes on millionaires and billionaires. Do they expect any other result? It is another sad "us-against-them" symptom of the sick class warfare dialogue. I wonder how Warren Buffett would have felt about the President's Buffett Plan before he became a billionaire. As an aside, wouldn't it be nice if Mr. Buffett would concentrate Berkshire Hathaway's holdings exclusively in companies that don't outsource employees or employ foreign workers by the hundreds of thousands? Are there any such companies?

Why don't we just cut to the chase and tax the upper class out of existence? If 70% of us believe that they need a higher rate, take it all and we will have to sink or swim without them. The dependent class will still be there and then we can see what we're entitled to. We should be focusing on the money we waste on the dependent class before looking to squeeze more from the 2%. They want to means-test higher income earners for Social Security and health care and never mention real need testing for dependent class entitlements.

THE MIDDLE CLASS FEEDS UPON ITSELF

Some of the 2% are probably scamming the system, too, but I have a hunch that the numbers are much smaller and the dollar amount much less than those who are scamming our healthcare, welfare, Medicaid, Social Security, and other so-called entitlement programs. As I mentioned earlier, there are no metrics to measure either easily—that's part of the problem. If we continue to go down this class-warfare road, this ginned-up populist rhetoric that fuels the flames of discontent will result in civil turmoil that may tear us apart as a nation. It's happening now as the disenchanted occupy everything from Wall Street and the Keystone Pipeline to Oakland, California. Thank you, Mr. President!

THE MIDDLE CLASS FEEDS UPON ITSELF

9 Our Legion of Lawyers

Some folks equate age with wisdom, but as I get older, it's obvious that they are wrong. Sure, as we get older, we do accumulate a boatload of knowledge about a lot of subjects, but the truth is that experience brings wisdom—at least when practical matters are considered. I go back to reading those advertisements about building that FM radio receiver when I was in my early twenties. If my brother could do it, anyone could do it! The reading was easy, but when I got the kit in the mail and opened the box, I knew I was in trouble. With a lot of help from a friend I managed to get through the multicolored spaghetti wire, transistors, capacitors and other small bits and pieces. It worked for a while before shutting down, but once was enough. The same goes for music, basement remodeling, and some car repairs. I've tried them, understand the complexities and my limitations, and have the wisdom to not try any of them again.

The wisdom came from doing. As we get older, our practical experiences expand our ability to solve problems and make decisions. The more we actually do things and solve problems, the more wisdom we acquire. I understand now why practice makes perfect and why some believe that those who can, do and those who can't, teach. How can we look to a President and Congress, few of whom have any practical experience in hiring or firing—other than office personnel—for solutions to our jobs crisis?

Unfortunately, Congress consists primarily of old white Christian men. The landscape of the 113th Congress has changed somewhat with an historic infusion of non-Caucasians and women, but it still remains old and white. The average of the 113th Congress has gone down by one year. The 113th House's average age is 56 years old vs.57 for the 112th. The 113th Senate's average age is 61 vs. 62 for the 112th.

The *CQ Roll Call Guide* to the 113th Congress indicates that law is the primary profession of Senators, followed by public service or politics, and business. Business is first In the House, then public service or politics, and law.

Some of the other professions represented in the 113th Congress, include:

• One hundred two teachers, professors and other education oriented professions.

• Nineteen physicians and five nurses.

• Five ordained ministers.

• Five Peace Corps volunteers.

• Three sheriffs and one deputy sheriff, two FBI agents, and one firefighter.

• Nine accountants in the House and two in the Senate

• Twenty-eight farmers, ranchers, or cattle farm owners.

• Seven social workers.

THE MIDDLE CLASS FEEDS UPON ITSELF

It isn't hard to see that most of these people don't have the essential life experiences to solve our job crises. Lawyers, politicians, and educators aren't what we need to solve the problem. There is a lot of knowledge but not much wisdom. When this information sinks in, it's easy to understand why our President or legislators are unable to cope with our current job crisis. And it *is* a crisis. We have historic high unemployment that may be close to an actual unemployment rate close to 18% when all of the unemployed are included. Only about 63% of working-age Americans are employed—the lowest rate since 1978. You don't hear our President talking about this issue. This crisis is resulting in unprecedented economic turmoil.

The U.S. housing market crash continues and is in mild depression while our national, state, and local tax revenues are shrinking. While our legislators are wringing their hands in a quandary trying to figure out solutions, we continue to slide downward. We have elected, and continue to elect, a legion of lawyers to manage the public wealth, but they just don't have the practical experience to solve our problems. The reduced tax base is creating turmoil as jobs and wages are cut throughout local and state governments. Our national debt has caused paralysis in government. Our legion of lawyers has repeatedly taken us to the brink of economic chaos, only to do a quick- and short-term fix, kicking the can down the road to our children. Instead of a legion of lawyers, we need an army of accountants.

Both party leaders of the Senate have been in office for more than twenty-five years (Reid, twenty-six years and McConnell, twenty-eight years). The same holds true for Nancy Pelosi (twenty-six years) and Boehner (twenty-two years). I'm sorry, but twenty-five or twenty-two years on the re-election treadmill doesn't make me confident that they can lead their way out of a burning barn, let alone out of our jobless crisis. Someone was using common sense when they limited the President to eight years in office but somehow lost it when not doing the same to our legislators.

Using the Internet, you'll find that there are currently about 1,100,000 lawyers in America and that about 90,000 of them are in Washington, DC. There must be at least 30,000 more in the Washington, DC area. I can't find the information, but there probably is at least half again that number serving in local and state governments, so I estimate that at least 10%, and probably more like 20%, of the nation's lawyers are mucking up the system in Washington and local and state governments. There are an incalculable number of lawyers working for the private sector attempting to influence and cope with government at all levels. To put it into perspective, there are fewer than one million physicians. No wonder we are in such trouble.

Instead of lawyers, we would be better off with accountants, but for the time being, we are stuck, with a collection of old elite men and women in both the executive and legislative branches of our government. Most are career politicians with little or no practical experience regarding job creation other than those created through the pork they have garnered for their districts through the old and ugly earmark system. Our President, a lawyer and teacher, is just like the rest of them. They have become a quasi-ruling elite class with little or no connection to the average American who sees his income diminish while the majority of our legislators have become millionaires—now that's progress.

Presidential hopeful and the Governor of Mississippi was on FOX News Sunday one morning. The commentator was questioning Barbour's low polling at a recent straw poll for the Republican nominee for President in 2012. His response was, of course, obfuscation but remarkable in what he considers the merits of his being President. To paraphrase his remarks, "With me you get a lobbyist, a politician, and a lawyer—it's a trifecta." Come on! None of these "occupations" make me feel good about his ability to represent me. Give me a business manager, an accountant, and a minister—that would be a real trifecta.

Our Congress is made up predominantly of old men and women. They work three days a week during most of the year, take off a month in the summer during a national crisis, and spend too much of their time working at getting re-elected. It's no wonder that they are disconnected with what could be called the average American's life. If age brought wisdom, all of our problems should be solved. Instead, when jobs are concerned, our elected representatives are impotent. When was the last time you went to a lawyer when you needed a job?

Do you know the joke about what's lower than whale &*#t? Just kidding!

THE MIDDLE CLASS FEEDS UPON ITSELF

10 Individualize Pension, Health & Welfare—Give Me a Bill

The current political consensus is leaning toward the belief that health care and Social Security for all Americans is a birthright. If that's where we're headed, we need to get healthcare off of the back of American employers. I look at social security as a general term that encompasses a lot of other services other than our Social Security pension program. What birthright means is hard for me to understand. If it means that all Americans—and is that American citizens or anyone who happens to be born in America or is it every person that happens to be here, whether legally or not, have the birthright? It's one of those political "feel good" terms that no one wants to define. If we want to be competitive in the world, we need to get healthcare and Social Security out of both the private and public employee benefit packages.

The rollout of The Affordable Care Act has been a disaster. Not only did the website crash and burn, but young healthy Americans did not seem to be signing up in the large numbers needed for its success. The act is so complicated that we won't know the real cost of the ACA for years.

The terrible design of the website certainly illustrates the inability of bureaucrats to implement complicated projects. How could they not know that traffic on the site would be in the millions? How could they not have tested it for months? How could they not protect the sensitive information required of applicants? The simple answer to these questions is that, except for the political backlash to the President and some legislators and the waste of taxpayer monies, the failure has had no career consequences. The President should have given the project to The National Security Agency. Just enter your phone number, e-mail address or the last four numbers of your social and the NSA would complete your application in detail, select your appropriate plan and deduct the premium from your bank account. It knows how to get stuff done.

As it's better known, Obamacare overlaid government-required benefits like guaranteed insurance for pre-existing conditions and the extension of dependent coverage to age twenty-six over existing plans. Well, as the saying goes, "it doesn't take a rocket scientist" to figure out that it would be very expensive.

American healthcare costs are shrouded in a dense fog caused by too many controversies. The debate continues over how the drug companies make excessive profits, how the public has no control over costs, and how our legion of lawyers drives up costs with malpractice suits. All are true. Most Americans believe it. Politicians will debate, haggle, protect their campaign donors, and obfuscate over the issue without any real regard to the cost to American employers, workers, and taxpayers. How funny is it to watch a commercial from a drug company selling a product for increasing low testosterone in men followed by another from an attorney looking for men who have been injured by the same type of drug?

Depending on the measurements, the quality of

the American healthcare system and its availability is arguably the best in the world. Unfortunately, it is probably the most expensive. We can blame it on the greedy healthcare industry, attorneys, and even the American public for causing the high cost of the system—it really doesn't matter. What matters for jobs is to put it in the public domain and take it off of the negotiation table between employers and unions, or government employees and taxpayers. By public domain, I don't mean a government healthcare program—the failure of the British and Canadian plans to provide our level of availability and quality at a much higher tax burden to their citizens should scare everyone.

One of our major problems is that those fortunate enough to have employer-provided, or are able to purchase health insurance, are paying for some of those who aren't so fortunate. Many of those individuals should really be part of our country's Social Security umbrella. We open our emergency rooms to anyone—as we should—but the costs for the uninsured get rolled into the costs of the insured and all taxpayers. Obamacare may change it, but there are too many Americans who believe that a healthcare policy is a luxury. Too many Americans roll the dice regarding healthcare and rely on our benevolent society to protect them if they develop a serious illness.

When an employer or governing unit sees the cost of healthcare go up, something has to give. Either the provider or purchaser absorbs the cost or transfers all or some of it to the worker or taxpayer. A recent article by the publisher of our local paper, *The Englewood Sun*, noted that the cost to the paper for family coverage is approximately $20,000 per year and is likely to rise to $40,000 in the next seven years. It's no wonder that many employers are trying to off-load healthcare costs to employees.

A good number of employers like Walmart seem to have a policy to employ as many part-time employees as possible to avoid providing reasonable benefits. Can you blame them? Is it no wonder that cities like Detroit are overburdened by the high cost of both healthcare and pension benefits to public employees? In my experience, negotiation between employees and employer are usually conducted under adversarial conditions. What is adversarial about a politician negotiating with the huge voting blocs those teacher and public service employee unions represent?

If it *is* a birthright, healthcare should be easily defined. It should be a basic program for all Americans from cradle to grave that keeps our excellent delivery system in place. It should be government regulated, not government administered. Anecdotal experiences that I have discussed with both British and Canadian friends lead me to believe that while their basic care is okay, many of them purchase additional private insurance to get delivery that still isn't as good or as readily available as ours. Many are irate when the public system is overloaded and the patients are shuffled into the private system.

Of course the big and debated questions for us are who pays, when we do pay, how we pay, can you opt out, and what is included. In my mind, healthcare and pension should be individualized. Every American should have to pay for his or her individualized—but government-regulated—pension and their basic individualized—but government regulated—health care plan.

THE MIDDLE CLASS FEEDS UPON ITSELF

Individualizing healthcare is complicated and a little bit scary. It's really complicated because of the myriad of special-interest groups involved in the process. First, there is the government, including state, local, and federal, none of which makes anything easy. Then we have physicians, insurance companies, drug companies, hospitals, employers, and the ever-present attorneys. Oh yes, then there's us, the taxpaying patients—and we pay for everything. There's also another special-interest group that no one likes to talk about and that is comprised of millions of Americans, many of whom cannot afford healthcare and many who can afford it, but who take their chances in gaming the system.

A universal healthcare plan needs to put the needs of the bureaucrats and special-interest groups behind the needs of the millions of users who pay their way. There has been a lot of discussion about whether there should be an individual mandate--financial prudence and common sense dictate that there should be. It's easy to say that mandatory healthcare is an issue of freedom of choice. The trouble is that in all too many cases, someone's freedom of choice results in draining public funds when one who chooses to opt out has not prepared for medical emergencies. Too often, people choose to have the most expensive cable package and the latest cell phone or computer and then rely on the taxpayer when it comes to healthcare.

What we need instead of Obamacare is a basic plan that takes into account cost of services, age, lifestyle choices, and life expectancy. There has to be a factor that can express how the aging process increases an individual's requirement for services. I'm sure that government and private industry actuaries can figure it out. A starting point would be a nominal plan that would include the basic necessary services required for an average American in average health over his or her lifetime. It would be the same plan for everyone over twenty-six years old. He or she would pay the premium from age twenty-six to a reasonable retirement age, eliminating both Medicare and Medicaid as we know them. The premium should reflect the unique male and female risks, marital status and regional variances. A basic mandatory plan can't be too hard to figure out. The biggest drawback to this type of system would be how to pay or account for the dependent class.

A twenty-year-old starting out in the workplace usually doesn't need a lot of healthcare. The least of my concerns at that age was healthcare. The fact that I worked for companies that provided a good health plan was nice but unimportant. Given the choice, I would probably have taken the money instead of the benefit. Most of us don't start annual physicals until we are well into our forties. Unfortunately, long before our forties many of our future health issues could be determined and prevented with early physicals, along with genetic and lifestyle screenings. Some schedule of required checkups and follow-ups should be part of a universal healthcare plan to help keep costs under control.

Once the requirements of the basic plan such as deductibles and co-pays, if any are determined, let insurance companies use their networks and compete for customers in the various regions of the country. The basic plan in New York City may cost more or less than the basic plan in Kansas City, so just tell me what it's going to cost. Deduct the payment from my check each week or each month before taxes or let me make a direct payment, but don't give it to the government.

THE MIDDLE CLASS FEEDS UPON ITSELF

Let me choose an independent but regulated insurance company and send it to them. Let me shop for additional increased coverage if I want it. If my employer chooses to supplement my costs, let them give it to me in wages so as not to complicate things. It would be a better method than to tax products and services as some countries do. Sure, the Canadians and Brits are in love with government-provided health care, but it isn't free and many have private plans purchased or provided by employers to supplement the national systems.

Taking out the entrenched special-interest groups is the only way to make a universal healthcare plan affordable and make it work. I'm on Medicare and take two generic medications each day. Neither of my two drugs costs me more than $10 per month. My insurance company allows me to purchase only a thirty-day supply of either of them unless I go online or call their central fulfillment company. If I use either method, they'll allow me to buy a ninety-day supply delivered to my home. Now these aren't exotic or expensive drugs—one is for my thyroid and the other is for cholesterol. I don't think either of them would bring a premium on the street drug market. I'll never understand the logic that prevents me from buying a year's supply of either medication and negotiate with my local pharmacy for a better price. Why do I even need a prescription?

If I go to my pharmacy and make the mistake of ordering the drugs too early, the druggist, forced by the insurance, drug company, or government rule, will reduce the number of pills by two or three and I end up with a twenty-seven-day supply. It's a small irritant to be sure, but it's indicative of a convoluted bureaucracy run by special-interest groups.

One of the topics in the Obamacare discussions was end-of-life issues and how they impact the cost of the program in general. There's no denying the fact that end-of-life care is expensive. It could be that with everyone having access to a managed healthcare system, we would be healthier and reduce end-of –life care costs. We can certainly figure out the cost for an average American and include it in the basic premium.

It is disheartening to talk to someone from England when the topic comes up. Many drugs available here are not available within their national health system. Many procedures such as hip and knee replacements that our elderly take for granted take months, or even years, before a senior can get them in England. Many are available on an expedited basis if they go through their private system. Somehow, the denial of these procedures to the elderly seems contrary to our expectations from a benevolent system. Are we to turn our backs on seniors?

We, as a nation, must solve the issue of universal healthcare. We need to do it in a manner that maintains quality, is reasonably affordable and reflects our values,

Our current method of providing Social Security is a 1930s approach to the new century worker that isn't working, given the changes in our society. We give the government buckets of money and they spend it by the bushel basket. The spending is in a fog that's incomprehensible to the average American. We need to divide and separate the current Social Security system into three areas—pension, health care, and—for lack of a better term—dependent class entitlements or welfare.

Pension should be much easier than health care. I

worked for more than fifty years and ended up with a 401(k) plan that was rolled into a self-directed IRA. Although regulated by the government, they kept their greedy hands from controlling it. I received yearly, and then monthly, statements from the onset of the plan. I couldn't take money out without paying taxes or penalties to the IRS. We would be much better off if our Social Security payments and the employer match, just as 401(k) plan monies do, went into a private account with rigid government regulations.

The money would be invested only in U.S. government bonds or their equivalent and be untouchable until retirement. In addition, if an employer or employee chose to put additional pre-tax monies into the account, a separate fund in the account would allow more investment options as are available in most IRA and 401(k) plans. President Obama has suggested the MyRA for all Americans. I believe it's terrific, but if we transferred the Social Security payments from employees and employers to individualized IRAs, with the additional account that would follow current guidelines for such accounts, Americans would be in control of their retirement options.

If a person starts at age twenty, making the current minimum wage $7.25 per hour or $15,080 per year and gets a 2% raise each year, they'll be earning $17.65 per hour, or $36,762.84 per year at age sixty-five. If they contribute 7% of their pay before taxes, and their employer contributes a matching 7%, they'll have accumulated almost $237,000 in their retirement account if they earn the same 2% on their money. The 2% growth rate for both income and interest rates is low but reflects current rates. Any increase in interest rates would make a significant impact on the accumulated nest egg. At 5% it would accumulate to around $310,000

The $237,000 would buy an annuity of $13,200 per year until age ninety. Even if purchasing an annuity were mandatory, the money would be there. The important point is that the money would be out of the government's hands and in control of the individual rather than of some bureaucrat. It wouldn't be forfeited if a person should die at age sixty-seven but would be available to his or her heirs. How often do we hear of an individual who retires at age sixty-five, only to die two years later and receive $250 as a Social Security burial benefit? Where do the funds go that he and his employers contributed in our current system? They probably go to the dependent class.

These individual accounts would be the core of an American's retirement planning. Any additional monies contributed by the employee or his employers could be invested in the other account with the same rules as current 401(k) and IRA accounts. Instead of the current system where the government gives you projections regarding your Social Security benefits somewhere around age fifty-five, individuals would get monthly or quarterly statements from their chosen retirement plan administrator, just as millions of American now receive from their 401(k) and IRA accounts.

All individuals and employers would be required to contribute the 7% without a cap on the amount of income earned. If a college graduate starts with a wage of $20 an hour, the accumulated monies are greater than $650,000 at age sixty-five. Of course, there are caveats: continued employment, the ability of government to keep their hands off the money, and

THE MIDDLE CLASS FEEDS UPON ITSELF

minimal government intervention in the process.

It is incomprehensible that so many Americans fear the privatization of Social Security and are content to let some lawyer or bureaucrat in Washington determine their financial destiny. Evidently, they fear corporations but want to work for one. They would rather throw money into the black hole that is our current Social Security system than take personal control of their retirement finances. But with the decline of defined benefit retirement plans and the growth of 401(k) types of plans, Americans are becoming more involved with, and knowledgeable about, retirement planning.

The trouble with implementing such a system is how to continue the existing payment of benefits once a change is made to personal responsibility. The current plan relies on active workers funding the benefits of retired workers. It may be hard to figure out, but such a plan would certainly be more relevant to today's worker. I believe we should put a plan in effect immediately for young Americans entering the workforce. We would then need to quantify the cost of the current program for those already in the existing program. Sure, it'll be difficult but not impossible.

So give me two bills, one for my personal individualized but government-regulated pension and one for my individualized but government-regulated health care plan. Make it a bill that I can understand and that covers my individual costs. Most working Americans should have no problem with this system and employers would love it. Then give me another bill, whether it's called charity, welfare, or—God forbid—my payment for the dependent class. Give me a bill for those who legitimately need help and those that suck on the system and enjoy benefits garnered from every employed American taxpayer's labors. No one wants to talk about it, but everyone who works and pays taxes pays for them. Give the guy flipping hamburgers at McDonald's a bill for the guy who elects to stay home and collect welfare. Give them a bill for the guy who elects to sell drugs and walks into the emergency room with a gunshot wound and no insurance. The dependent class is killing us, but nobody wants to talk about it, certainly not our politicians and the high and mighty who have no connection to the average American's day-to-day struggle.

A recent NPR program highlighting the—for a lack of a better description—convoluted processes involved with our Social Security disability system should enrage all working Americans. You can view the entire report at http://apps.npr.org/unfit-for-work/. There are fourteen million Americans on disability. That is two million more than are unemployed. These fourteen million are effectively absent from unemployment statistics. The Social Security disability system is crowded with attorneys who are making millions of dollars of taxpayer money. The report sites one firm collecting $68,000,000 in fees. There are companies used by states to get people off of welfare rolls and move them onto disability in order to shift the expense away from the states to the federal government. Of course, states have to balance their budget whereas the federal government doesn't. I don't believe anyone can accurately determine how much we spend on this and other "social programs" that aren't monitored or policed by anyone. If only we could get a detailed bill.

11 End the Wars

The War on Drugs

According to the Office of National Drug Control Policy, our President requested $25.6 billion for fiscal year 2013 to support evidence-based drug control programs—an increase of about $14.5 million, and that's just for federal programs

The U.S. prison population is about 2.3 million. More than half a million of the prisoners are incarcerated for drug law violations. Any Internet search engine will reveal the appalling facts on the war on drugs. I hate to say "Google it" because Google is one of those too-big-to-succeed-for-our-own-good entities that is destroying jobs in America, so use another search engine. It's near impossible to come up with the true costs of the war. There are hundreds of Internet sites, even one with a clock "www.drugsense.org/wodclock.htm" that is constantly updated with Federal and State spending on the war. The spending is mind-boggling, and if you go to this site, you can find government figures by function and department http://www.whitehousedrugpolicy.gov/publications/policy/10budget/index.html

What none of the sites captures is the costs not usually associated with the war on drugs.

Most Americans are paying their law enforcement and related personnel a wage premium due to this war. It's typical during wage negotiations for law enforcement and related positions for negotiators to cite wages paid in major cities, or national averages that are highly influenced by major city pay rates. There are more than 900,000 law enforcement officers in the U.S. A New York City policeman makes close to $80,000 per year after five years on the job, and it's a dangerous job. How much of the danger is caused by drug-related crime? If you take the 900,000 law enforcement officers in the country and use a low number of $10,000 as the average danger wage premium, we taxpayers pay for the danger factor caused by drug-related crimes at the tune of nine billion dollars per year, year after year after year!

This danger premium is not limited to police officers. It also goes to Emergency Medical Technicians, firemen, and other public servants involved with keeping the public safe. I knew a guy who worked as an EMT in Chicago who said it was typical, when entering some Chicago projects, to be shot at by the druggies and gang members living in the apartments. Many times, they would have to get a local minister to accompany them when answering an emergency call. It was, and still is, a dangerous job with a high-danger premium included in their pay rates. Of course, all American taxpayers pay this premium, whether they are real estate, sales, or other taxes imposed by governing bodies.

What about the tax dollars that are spent providing medical and welfare services to those individuals who are either victims of the war on drugs or because they are associated with dealers or users who are not direct victims? How many men, women, and children are dumped into the public welfare system because of the war on drugs? How much of our health care costs is due to the burden they place on our hospitals and other medical facilities? How many husbands, wives, mothers, and fathers who are imprisoned because of the war on drugs leave behind dependents who must be provided for by the American taxpayer? Could any of the homeless across America be victims of drug abuse?

So we pay this danger premium to our law enforcement personnel around the country, and they deserve it and now, our prisons are overloaded with the results of their labor. I don't believe anybody knows the real percentage of our prison population that is related, either directly or indirectly, to the drugs issue. Many of the statistics are black and white. A criminal is in prison for drug dealing, drug possession, or for a crime committed while under the influence of drugs and other such easily-categorized offenses. No one can say how many are imprisoned due to socio-economic conditions created by drug use.

Instead of having a war on drugs, we need to legalize and tax all drugs as we do alcohol and tobacco. It makes no sense whatsoever to criminalize drugs while alcohol use is legal and, in many cases, glorified through advertisements. We have spent billions advertising alcohol and many, many more billions trying to stamp out drug use. It makes more sense to have growers, manufacturers, users, and sellers of drugs monitored and taxed instead of continuing our endless and fruitless efforts to stop drug trafficking. How can we rationally moralize that one is good and the other is bad? Unfortunately, the net result would probably be a reduction in law enforcement personnel and lower wages, but

Andy Leonard

fortunately, the bill to the American taxpayer would be a lot lower. A good step in the right direction is the Attorney General's current instruction to federal prosecutors to drop mandatory minimum sentencing in some drug cases. I'd like to see the day when Maui Wowie is advertised along with Bud Light in a Super Bowl commercial. A better step is the recent legalization of marijuana in Colorado and other states.

And we must take moral responsibility for the thousands of Mexicans who have been murdered by drug cartels and gangs engaged in transporting drugs to America. We're fighting a war in the Middle East where poppy growers, whose product ends up in the U.S. as heroin, support some of our enemies. Sure, drugs are bad but so is the excessive or violent use of tobacco, alcohol, and guns. But the death and destruction caused by our appetite for illegal drugs is really, really bad. At $125 or more per ounce, the trafficking in marijuana is certainly a cause for a large number of gun-related crimes. Once Americans are allowed to grow the stuff on their own property, the price will plummet and I believe weed-related crime will do the same.

Would we rather fight the war with guns and prisons, or quit and address the problems of abuse with legalization and treatment as we do with alcohol?

Middle-East Wars

We fail our moral compass and ignore the more-than-twenty-thousand Mexicans killed as a result of drug wars, primarily as the result of our country's appetite for illegal drugs, and then we turn around and spend billions on wars in countries vital to the drug trade. Are we really expecting to change ancient tribal and religious enmities that have resulted in an incalculable amount of deaths and maiming? It's no wonder that many countries stand aside and look at us as fools and allow us to squander American lives and resources on wars that won't change their conditions in the long run. We're fighting, and our men and women are dying, in countries where poppy cultivation is helping to finance our so-called enemies.

The Middle East is in Europe's back yard, and yet we were embroiled in two wars there without much European support. Kabul is twice as far from Washington DC as it is from Paris, yet our legion of lawyers sends our sons and daughters to fight a battle that somehow was rationalized by the 9-11 attacks on our country. When we quit the wars, nothing major will change. We aren't making friends in the Middle East with the wars. A disinterested Europe offers little help and support from our "friends," is minimal. The future of the Middle East will have a far greater impact on England, Europe, and Africa than on America, yet we continue to be the lead dog expending the precious lives of our American youth. We spent billions of dollars on the Iraq war, only to see tribal and sectarian violence erupt again. Hardly a week goes by without some religious zealot blowing his or herself up along with dozens of others. Isn't it about time that we say "enough is enough?"

The lost war in Viet Nam continues to haunt the American psyche. What did we gain from the deaths of American men and women? Could it be the low cost of shirts selling at Walmart? I know some Viet Nam vets who cringe and get ugly when the subject comes up. We are selling patriotic hats made in Viet Nam and ten years from now, we'll probably be buying the same hat made in Afghanistan, but our legion of lawyers continues to get us embroiled in conflicts that drain our economy and put Americans in harm's way. Well, the coffers are empty and too much blood has been spent. Enough is enough!

The War on Poverty

For fifty years, America has been warring on poverty with little success. From 19% in 1964 when President Johnson introduced the Economic Opportunity Act, the poverty rate has fluctuated dramatically but was at 15% in 2011. Like the war on drugs, the war on poverty as we are fighting it isn't winnable. What we have is a welfare-providing bureaucracy that many feel has morphed into an unmanageable and ineffective system. Like most government efforts, it's impossible to measure and therefore, we can't manage the effort. Unfortunately, the only measure we have is the number of Americans below the poverty level, and this number is dismal.

It's too easy to rant about the number of people on food stamps, housing assistance, and other forms of government handouts but no one offers an alternative. There are some, but a legion of lawyers doesn't have the will to implement them. We continue to use the same tools over and over to end poverty and expect different results. It's the definition of insanity.

12 Government Changes in Attitudes

The American public loves to hate lawyers and politicians. Unfortunately, many—if not most—politicians are lawyers. The following joke that everyone knows says it all: How can you spot a lawyer or a politician walking down the street? He'll have his hands in someone else's pockets. More often than not, the hands are in our—the taxpayers'—pockets.

The lawyers, politicians, and government employees provide the sludge that now mucks up the system. Nothing is getting done. They have a penchant for creating massive documents they don't take the time to read and building a bureaucracy that's inefficient at best. They're parasites on the body of the American taxpayer. Instead of enabling, they disable. Instead of being functional, they're frictional. Instead of a government of the people, by the people, and for the people, we have a government of, by, and for the special interest groups that finance or influence our political electoral process.

Just look at how bureaucrats have screwed up air travel in a quest to protect us. We get to the airport two hours early, wait in endless lines, take off our shoes, throw away contraband, go through metal detectors, submit to touch searches and body scans, and schlep our bags from security to boarding gates, all due to a bizarre system that can be streamlined and made efficient. If safety is the goal, why not focus on the vulnerable baggage and make it faster and easier to get on an airplane?

If everyone were required to check all of their bags at the entrance to the airport at no charge, the airlines would be required to handle bags securely and efficiently. Since most airlines started charging for checked bags, the overhead bins and under-seat storage areas are packed. Now some are also charging for carry-on bags. It stands to reason that as more bags and packages get into the cabin, chances are that something dangerous such as the new printed plastic guns will get through the check-in lines, putting passengers at increased peril. It was interesting that, on a recent trip from Florida to Kansas City, I heard one of the baggage handlers saying how easier it would be to board the planes if carry-on bags were limited.

Limiting cabin baggage would probably cut the boarding process by more than half. Why do we allow someone traveling from Chicago to Cleveland to bring a suitcase, briefcase, and computer into the cabin? Is their time so valuable that they can't check their bags and get them at the baggage claim area? They waste time rummaging through the overhead storage bins trying to squeeze a fourteen-inch bag into a twelve-inch opening while the rest of us unimportant passengers wait for them to get through.

It would be a lot safer and less expensive for American taxpayers if every seat on the plane had a basic computer and if passengers were limited in what they were allowed to carry on board. What about a see-through plastic box that could go through the scanner and nothing else? Put in a book, flash stick,

THE MIDDLE CLASS FEEDS UPON ITSELF

cell phone, Game Boy, and any other essential travel item and be done with it. Instead of charging for checked bags, charge a hefty fee for extra bags brought into the cabin, and make those who elect to do so arrive much earlier and go through an extensive search. The few passengers with special needs could be addressed separately or asked to arrive early.

Planes would be safer, board faster, and leave on time. Airlines would be forced to handle bags efficiently. We bitch and moan about the current process, but we are part of the problem. American Airlines recently started testing to allow passengers without carry-on bags to board early—what a thought! Unfortunately, it'll make more room for the idiots to bring more bags into the cabin.

Our government is ever expanding. Instead of trying to do more with less, they seem to be trying to do more while asking for more and treating the American taxpayer like a patsy. The recent trouble in the housing markets was a terrible awakening to local governments. Housing values plummeted, and along with the decline in housing prices came a sharp decrease in the tax base. Optimistically, most local governments expected prices to return and did nothing. True to form, many first steps were to increase rates in order to maintain the status quo. As the impact became greater, the hope that the tax dollars would soon come back to their previous levels kept bureaucrats from taking decisive action, and reduced services came next. Things kept getting worse until finally, consolidation of departments and decreasing headcount became the solution. The process was long in many cases and the reduced tax base may last for years.

The same process occurs in business in a much more condensed timeframe. What businesses, except very large ones, can continue for three or four years with declining sales or revenue and remain viable? Not many. If the business is going to succeed, there needs to be something left after expenses are subtracted from sales. Usually, the first step is to reduce headcount and rehire only if absolutely necessary. In government, the goal is not to have anything left over—use it or lose it—and that's the rub. It's a difficult attitude to change if there's no incentive to have anything left over once the cost of services is subtracted from the tax base.

In government, if there's anything left over, the answer is to expand services, whether they're necessary or not. Until recently, they very seldom planned for a rainy day or decreased taxes. The election process doesn't help either. How often have you heard a politician brag about reduced spending or cost cutting? These words aren't in their lexicon. It isn't how they get elected and re-elected. They get elected by doing more for their constituents and that works only if the tax well doesn't run dry. The recent tax drought has caused a little change in their attitude and hopefully, circumstances will change the tax-and-spend attitude to one of fiscal responsibility.

Go on the Internet and read the mission statements of government agencies and cities. Can you tell me why they need a mission statement at all? You won't find many where their only goal is to deliver acceptable services to taxpayers at the lowest possible cost. Instead, the mission statements are loaded with niceties and have a "feel good" quality. Tax dollars were spent to have someone compose these written monstrosities and to tweak them from time to time, but when the tax cutter comes, these mission statements may ring false. The public servants of America need as their primary goal that a major part of their mission—the most important part—is to save taxpayer money. Of course, many include the word "efficient" in the statement, but what they should use instead is the phrase "achieving the desired result with the minimum use of time, effort, and taxpayer money."

Most of the mission statements have a very friendly tone, but are they necessary? Many of them use the phrase "exceed expectations." All I want from my local government is to meet my expectations, not exceed them. The cost of exceeding expectations is just too much for taxpayers to bear!

Typical of Congress is their wrangling, wheeling, and dealing in their attempt to cut the current deficit and as usual, they look to raise taxes on someone or some class of taxpayer. Any good CEO running a company knows the answer. Run the government like a business; consolidate, eliminate, and scrutinize all operations; and more importantly, change the attitudes of our public servants.

If you look at the mission and vision statements that seem to have become a requirement of every public office, you seldom see the idea that they should be providing acceptable services at the lowest possible cost to taxpayers. Instead, they all want to "exceed our expectations" with little regard for cost. We need a drastic attitudinal shift of our public servants. Instead of what else can we do with our tax dollars, they need to be constantly thinking of how to do more with less. We send them money by the bucket and they spend it by the bushel.

Too often, we see public servants attempting to expand their spheres of influence in order to justify more employees, bigger budgets, and expanded but unnecessary services. The sad reduction in newspapers across the country is diminishing the scrutiny of government at all levels. Who or what will replace the magnifying glass of professional investigative journalists? Taxpayers need a budget ombudsperson constantly looking at costs, organization, and efficiencies—someone whose job it is to look at government as a business. If we can start doing it at the local level where many politicians begin their careers, it may force the change of attitude that we need in our state and federal governments.

Our local county government where we live in southwest Florida is typical. It is an area that welcomes snowbirds in the winter and is kind of slow and easy the other six or seven months of the year. Hurricane Charley hit the area in the August of 2004. The local FEMA manager wanted to, and did, put up indicators on all stop signs throughout our area showing in what flood zones residents are located so they know when to leave. The initial cost was minimal, but the reasoning for doing it was questionable. Forget the fact that most residents buy hazard and flood insurance that is rated on your wind and flood zone. Forget that just about everyone has a computer and can get the information from the Internet. Forget that we get a week's notice that major storms are coming. Forget that regardless of what flood zone in which you're located, common sense tells you to get out of Dodge when a storm is on the way. And yet, many local residents think it was a worthwhile project without questioning the cost of maintaining it or whether it was even necessary.

They also want to spend millions creating or improving evacuation roads instead of using common sense and making them one way out of the area when a storm is on the way. The laughable aspect of their willingness to spend our money is that during hurricane season, our area population is greatly reduced by the absence of snowbirds. When Charley hit, the locals were standing in grocery checkout lines holding maps printed from the NOAA storm-tracking site and got out of the area without clogging the adequate evacuation roads. Those who stayed would have stayed regardless of the colored band on local stop signs. It was a given that they would proceed with the signs and road projects instead of saving the money. It's all about attitude.

The local paper wanted Florida to get some of the seed money to run a bullet train from Orlando to Tampa. This is hysterical! What's the wisdom behind a high-speed rail between Tampa and Orlando? Other than to join the madness to trumpet all things green, it makes no sense. We get a 1.9 billion federal tax windfall. Terrific! When the oil companies get a windfall, it's terrible, but we get a windfall from the American taxpayer and it's grand? Whoopee!

Can you see it? A family of four goes to Orlando from Tampa. They call a cab to take them to the station or drive their car to the station and pay to park. Schlepping bags, they buy four tickets and enjoy the short trip to Orlando. They get a taxi or limo to the hotel or rent a car—you can't get around Orlando or many of our big cities very well without a car. Or they can drive their car door to door the ninety miles for

Andy Leonard

about ten gallons of gas and have the convenience of their car. Other than to save about an hour, why would they do it and how often?

It isn't surprising that Ohio, the place of my birth, and Wisconsin turned down the taxpayer windfall. Cleveland to Columbus by high-speed rail—all aboard? America isn't Spain or China. We have the most vehicles per capita than any other country and one of the highest home ownership rates. These two factors, along with the vastness of America, have resulted on average in the best roads in the world. It's foolish to suggest that we're going to get out of our cars and hop the train to destinations where having a car is essential.

Our large cities have spread out, abandoning the central hubs that are more common in Europe. Most are far apart without much city-to-city commuting. They need urban mass transit, not high-speed rail. But even a city like Chicago with a good urban transit system still has hundreds of thousands of cars going daily from suburb to city or vice versa with only one occupant. They sit on the Kennedy Expressway, bogged down while the elevated train speeds by. Driving through Atlanta recently during morning commute time, the Heavily Occupied Vehicle lane was pretty much empty. There were very few heavily occupied vehicles. Most vehicles in the regular lanes were traveling faster than those in the HOV lanes.

High-speed rail is not right for most of America right now and it may never be. Like Europe and other densely populated countries, it makes sense in the northeast where the population is concentrated and there's heavy inter-city traffic, but not Florida, Ohio, or Wisconsin. That is a shotgun approach. We should

THE MIDDLE CLASS FEEDS UPON ITSELF

focus on the Boston, New York, and Washington areas or in some of the densely populated areas of California. Whether we like it or not, the automobile has become indispensable to Americans and we may still sit in our cars while the bullet train flashes by.

Despite our love affair with, and our reliance on, the automobile, high-speed rail might work in America. Instead of handing out billions of dollars to states like Ohio, Wisconsin, and Florida, give it all to the northeast and let them perfect it. Unfortunately, the dismal failure of Amtrak makes one grimace at the thought of government involvement in such a vital project. We don't need any more black holes into which to throw our tax dollars.

I got off point there, but it's all about the attitude of government employees at all levels. I keep thinking about the U. S. Postal Service. For many years, our postmen—and they were postmen—walked or rode by just about every home and business in the country. Their job was to deliver the mail through rain, sleet, hail, etc. without regard for cost, and they did it very well.

With just a little change in their attitude regarding costs and increasing services, the post office might not have lost the package-and-overnight business to Fed Ex and UPS. I know a lot of retired postal workers and they are proud of their service and of the post office's reliability. When I suggest to them that they should have been interested in expanding and giving better service and cutting costs, I get blank stares. Today, the postal service is operating in the red. Soon, elimination of Saturday delivery and massive layoffs will hit it. With the ability to receive and pay bills online, send e-mails around the world, and transmit what used to be printed matter to everyone, it's hard to visualize the postal service ten or even five years from now. You can be sure, though, that the unions and bureaucracy will fight to keep it going.

Here's a "what if" for the Post Office. What if it reduced mail service to homes to two days a week—Monday and Thursday, for example—and spent the rest of the time trying to get package and next-day delivery business away from UPS and FedEx? Technology is certainly reducing the necessity of next-day delivery, but there's a lot of package business out there. How about consolidating the Post Office with other government services like the Mint or military recriting? Unfortunately, to make any serious change might require an act of Congress. Good luck!

The following is purported to be an actual passport application letter sent back to the State Department. Even if it isn't, it certainly says something about our view of bureaucrats.

"Dear Mrs, Ms., or Sir:

"I am in the process of renewing my passport and still can't believe this. How is it that Radio Shack has my address and telephone number and knows that I bought a cable TV from them in 1987 (twenty- three years ago) and yet the federal government is still asking me where I was born and on what date?

For Christ sakes, do you guys do this by hand? Ever heard of computers? You have my birth date in my social security file is on EVERY income tax form I've filed for the past thirty years. It's on my Medicare health insurance card and my driver's license. It's on the last eight damn passports I've had,

THE MIDDLE CLASS FEEDS UPON ITSELF

It's on every stupid customs declaration form I've had to fill out before being allowed off the plane for the last thirty years. And it's on all those census forms that we have to do at election times.

Would somebody please take note once and for all that my mother's name is Maryanne, my father's name is Robert, and I'm reasonably confident that neither name is likely to change between now and when I die? Between you and me, I've had enough of this bureaucratic bullshit!You send the application to my house, then you ask me for my #*&#%*& address. What is going on? You must have a gang of bureaucratic Neanderthal morons working there!

Look at my damn picture. Do I look like Bin Laden? And no, I don't want to dig up Yasser Arafat, for shit sakes! I just want to go and park my ass on a sandy beach. And would someone please tell me, why would you give a damn whether I plan on visiting a farm in the next fifteen days? If I ever got the urge to do something weird to a chicken or a goat, believe you me, I'd sure as hell not want to tell anyone!

Well, I have to go now because I have to go to the other end of the city and get another #*@&#^@*@& copy of my birth certificate to the tune of $100. Would it be so difficult to have all the services in the same area so I could get a new passport the same day? Nooooo! That would require planning and organization and it would be too logical for the @&^*^%@% government.

You'd rather have us running all over the place

like chickens with our heads cut off. Then we have to find some asshole to confirm that it's really me in the damn picture. You know, the one where we're not allowed to smile. Hey, you know why we can't smile? We're totally pissed off!
Signed: An Irate Citizen

P.S.: Remember what I wrote about getting someone to confirm that the picture is me? Well, my family has been in the United States of America since 1776. I have served in the military for something over thirty-five years and have had security clearances up the ying yang. However, I have to get someone important to verify who I am. You know, someone like my doctor WHO WAS BORN AND RAISED IN INDIA!"

Unfortunately, items like the above garnered from the Internet are hard to authenticate but ring true to many of us. We need a basic change in attitude toward government at all levels. The best place to start would be local government—a microcosm of state and federal governments. Instead of lobbyists, we have interest groups. The ones with the biggest budgets or communication system, even though they don't comprise a majority of the population, hold sway over local politicians. If they aren't catered to, re-election could hang in the balance. Too often, the apathy of the majority of our eligible voters results in money being spent on items appealing to narrow pockets of our citizens.

Government should be, to use a phrase that guided the company I worked for most of my life, "a bare-bones operation." Instead, we suffer with politicians who, because of the system, are more concerned with being re-elected than with saving taxpayer dollars. I don't want them to exceed my expectations, just meet them.

We need a change in attitude of the elected and the electorate. The electorate needs to become involved with the day-to-day operations of government. We need to go to meetings, write local officials, and be more involved with their decisions. If we don't, the special-interest groups will run the government. They vote and contribute to election campaigns as a block. Local government needs to be more open and responsive to the majority but seldom heard from members of the electorate. A canned e-mail response from an elected official indicating how important our message was just doesn't cut it and reflects arrogance. Unfortunately, too many of us tolerate it. The head of the local Chamber of Commerce or teachers' union representative probably gets a personal response or a call. Until elected officials begin to be influenced by the average voter, fiscal responsibility will always be trumped by reelection strategy. The circus going on in Washington is the proof.

And after all, except for the largest of our cities, local government is the little league of American politics and state government is the minor league. The good ones progress through the farm system to the big leagues and big money, which Washington has become. Money becomes critical. They don't have to be good at governing; they have to be good at getting re-elected, and re-election is just almost always contingent upon the ability to raise money.

Special interests and their paid lobbyists with bags filled with cash become kingmakers and the average voter loses just about all influence. Governing becomes an occupation instead of a public service. The bureaucracy expands and our two political parties, which are just a conglomeration of different special interest groups, receive the largesse of the kingmakers, and the average voter becomes further removed from the process and loses influence.

We need to expect more for less rather than less for more. Better yet, the business of government. should be run like a business. If we start with our local governments and allow only the fiscally responsible members to progress through the system, we can surely change the big-money business that is Washington.

The Tea Party is the five-hundred-pound gorilla in our political circus right now. Unfortunately, many view it as a bunch of crackpots aligned with the far right and dismiss it as just another special-interest group. They missed the target in their strategy that aligned them with the Republican Party. In today's political world of white and black, left and right, big and small, and red states and blue states, they chose a road traveled by less than half the voters. We don't need a Tea Party, we need a We Party, with "we" being the average voter who works hard, balances a checkbook, and borrows when needed but responsibly. Had they taken the middle of the road traveled by the majority of responsible Americans, theirs would be a much easier journey.

13 Commit to America

Lately, it has become popular to compare America with other countries with regard to education, health. welfare and other social topics. Too often the comparison is to countries with small homogeneous populations like Finland and Sweden. The Nordic population is around twenty five million. Finland's is less than six million. Ours is three hundred plus million and not very homogeneous. We can and will excel with the right leadership and a plan to commit to America.

I'm sorry, but I listened to our lame duck President give a speech last year in Galesburg, IL, on the economy, and was disgusted. To be frank, it was more a campaign speech than an honest discussion of the economic reality facing the American worker. Evidently, he believes that pre-school education, immigration reform, lower interest rates on college loans, and the implementation of The Affordable Care Act will create jobs in America. Interspersed with his comments were the usual pot shots at the 2%, the deriding of Republican divisiveness, and his pandering to the middle class. My take was that the champion of the middle class is clueless and he further reinforced my opinion with his 2014 State of the Union address.

Instead of smooth speeches, we need a modern-day equivalent to the Works Progress Administration. But as the WPA focused on infrastructure and government projects, Commit to America would focus on creating private sector jobs and eliminating unnecessary, and often redundant, government jobs. It should be alarming to all of us that jobs in the private sector shrink and government employment increases. When we get blips up in employment, the cause is usually an increase in lower-paying service and retail jobs. As private sector jobs decrease, the dependent class gets larger while we create an ever-growing elite governing class. As government expands, we get more rules, more regulations, and more restrictions for both employers and private citizens. It's no wonder that American companies sit on their hoard of cash.

Getting the huge number of unemployed Americans back to work won't happen by investing in our infrastructure such as rebuilding roads, rails, dams, and other massive government projects. Their impact on jobs is short lived and requires long-term employed American taxpayers to finance them. Isn't the problem that we can't afford to maintain our existing infrastructure without enormous government borrowing? Instead of creating government jobs, our government should be facilitating the ability of the private sector to put people to work. Once that happens, infrastructure jobs will be able to be financed. It will put the horse in front of the cart.

We need to put more money in the average American's pocket. Maybe it wouldn't create a lot of new jobs, but it certainly would help the continued existence of jobs that are now in place. For many Americans—probably the majority—budget costs are more or less fixed or controllable. House payments, rent, insurance costs, utility bills, food costs, and car payments are fixed or can be managed somewhat. Some of the major items that affect most American's discretionary spending are the costs of gasoline, the cost of government, and of course, the availability of jobs. Our mission must be to create sustainable American jobs in the private sector and reduce the cost of government. In no special order, here are ways that I believe we can accomplish the mission

Rewrite the Tax Code

Our tax code is like an all-you-can-eat buffet for our legion of lawyers. Interpretation and application of the 74,000 pages it contains supports lawyers, lobbyists, and through their donations, many politicians. Because of this money circle of influence, the code is a goldmine for our legislators. Someone on a CNN show said that General Electric has over 800 tax lawyers working for it and to be sure, not many—if any—are working so that their client pays more taxes.

I remember the simplicity of my first returns. How much did I earn? How much did I owe? I was single with no dependents and no deductions, but now it's a different story. As a realtor, I get business deductions in addition to the interest and charitable and loss carryovers from bad investments that I get on my personal income. And I am semi-retired. Of course, contrary to my better judgment, I bypass any local tax preparer and use TurboTax. Next year, I vow to use one of the local tax preparers.

Jumping on a recent IRS scandal regarding nonprofit entities, the Tea Party is resurrecting its flat-tax proposal. I can't help but believe that a vast majority of Americans, if they really understood it, would be opposed to the concept of a flat tax. Let's just take every penny of earned income and tax it at an equitable rate without deductions. Tax corporations at a rate that is job creation friendly and discourages them from hiding money in other countries. Forget about the loopholes that have been inserted into the code by our elected representatives and apply the rates to all income. A hedge fund manager would pay the same rate as the cook and wait staff working at your local restaurant. I believe the only exceptions should be the money in individual personal retirement accounts and the cost of individual healthcare whether provided by an employer or paid for by individuals.

There is a Republican proposal to change the tax code that, among other steps, would reduce tax brackets to three, the highest of which would impose an extra 10% tax on those that earn over $450,000.00 per year. Even Republicans are now targeting the 2% in order to get popular support of an unfair tax system. Why penalize those of us who are more than likely to be the job generators in America?

The formula for a flat tax is simple. How much did I earn minus retirement and healthcare payments? How much do I owe minus how much income tax my employer deducted from my pay or how much did I prepay? Do the math and either send a check or get a refund. The IRS will be relegated to verifying income and tracking down discrepancies in reported income and monitoring Obamacare instead of applying the 74,000-page tax code.

I don't believe that the average American realizes the enormous amount of money that is being spent year after year by corporations and wealthy individuals to work the tax code to their favor. A good tax lawyer can be invaluable to a large company's CEO. To be sure, there's nothing wrong with the practice, particularly when the rewards can be huge and legal under the current tax code.

On the other hand, mortgage interest and real

estate tax payments are usually the biggest deductions available to most Americans. There is an honest fear that eliminating these deductions without ensuring a fair flat tax rate would be a disaster for the middle class. Some of the fear is fueled by many of those that have the most to fear from a flat tax—politicians, bureaucrats, and lawyers. I believe that a flat tax would result in a more efficient government, a more fair distribution of our tax burden, and that our political process would be less influenced by money. Utopia!

Declare war on oil prices.

Many households have two workers and two cars. The difference between two-dollar-per-gallon gas and four- or five-dollar-per-gallon gas can severely affect not only a family's discretionary spending, but also its ability to cover other expenses. We seem to have no defense against the rising and falling gasoline prices. A right direction would be to attack gasoline prices on every front.

There's no single great long-term solution. We must not dismiss a single project as the President has done with the Keystone pipeline because it will take some time to get results or may have an impact on the environment. The denial of Keystone indicates how crippled our efforts to solve our energy problem have become. It was, and continues to be, a politicized fiasco. And sure enough, in the continued politicization of Keystone the President has postponed the decision on the project until after the coming mid-term elections. Hope and Change—what?

A primary metric of job creation is the amount of money available to Americans for discretionary spending. We need to put more money in every American's pocket. An easy way to do that for many

Americans would be to reduce the price of a gallon of gas. We use more energy per capita than any other country in the world. We're the largest consumer of oil in the world, not mainly because we're greedy but because that's how our country developed, along with our lifestyle. Except for those of us who live and work in the large eastern metro areas like New York and Boston, or who commute using public transportation and don't have or need a car, we depend on gasoline to get from place to place.

One of the great government projects of America was the interstate highway system. You can go across the country from north to south and east to west on great roads, and we use them for commuting to work, travel, and for commerce. There are few countries in the world where you can drive 5,100 miles (Key West to Anchorage) and never cross another border or worry about your safety. It's why Americans drive more than most other Inhabitants of the planet.

Tell someone from England that you're driving 800 miles to see a relative and they'll be astonished. Tell them that you commute sixty miles one way back and forth to work, and they'll also be astonished. One of the highest taxes on the American public is the excessive price of a gallon of gasoline. Except for those living in the large urban areas across our country, most Americans are automobile junkies. We usually don't train, bus, subway, walk, bicycle, or helicopter from home to work—we drive. Again, it's just our way of life. We leave our hometowns for better jobs or milder climates. Living in Florida, it's not uncommon for our friends to drive 1,000 miles to see their families. We don't take trains because they're inconvenient and slow. Even if they were fast, we probably wouldn't use them because of our

THE MIDDLE CLASS FEEDS UPON ITSELF

dependence on, and love of, the automobile.

Get a bird's eye view of the Kennedy Expressway in Chicago and you'll see a symptom of the reality. There are hundreds of thousands of cars occupied by one person taking the highway to work. It's easy to blame them for not carpooling or taking the "elevated," but that's just the nature of most of our big cities. We had an urge to find open areas away from the congestion of the city where the dream of a family, house, and open spaces could come true, and for many of us, it did. At a dollar a gallon, the effect on most of us was minimal. At $3.50 to $4.00 a gallon, or a projected $5.00 a gallon, the dream is becoming a nightmare.

We fled the cities to the suburbs to find affordable homes and a better place to raise a family but still worked in the city. The relatively low price of gasoline actually made the outward migration easy. Gasoline under a dollar a gallon was little to pay in exchange for suburban life. As cities grew, so did the suburban sprawl, thus increasing the daily commute for many Americans. We continued to improve our roads to the suburbs to make the daily commute easier, putting millions of Americans on the highways from suburbs to the city, but the four-dollar-per-gallon gas has made the road bumpy. Our work ethic—get there early and stay late—is also a hindrance to car pooling and mass transit use. Your neighbor may work in the same area or building as you do but have a much different personal work schedule.

We will never get people off of the highway without a major change in our suburban lifestyle. Until that happens, if ever, we must make a serious effort to reduce the economic burdens that high gasoline prices place on all of us. At 12,000 miles per vehicle and 22 mpg in a two-vehicle family, a $1.00 reduction in the price of a gallon of gas would save over $1,000 for the family. Conversely, a $1.00 increase in the price of a gallon takes $1,000 out of families' discretionary spending and hurts its ability to cover other expenses.

Also, because of our demand for lower prices, we quit buying American-made products and energized foreign economies. As industries in Japan, India, and China grew, so did their consumption of gasoline, driving prices higher. China is putting millions of new drivers in automobiles each year, increasing world demand for oil. Again, we feed upon ourselves.

Supposedly, we are now getting most of our energy from North America and have increased our oil production over the past few years. Bill O'Reilly was ranting about the fact that as we produce more gasoline, we are exporting it rather than keeping it here and increasing supplies in America. That may be true, but it really doesn't make too much sense to keep it here just to satisfy our extravagant consumption. We must attack both sides of the supply/demand equation.

The best present solution to the demand side is either to get Americans off the highway through alternative methods of transportation or into efficient cars. Europeans have embraced the fuel-efficient diesel engine while Americans can't seem to get over the terrible failure of early diesel powered cars introduced decades ago. Providing an efficient transportation system that is fast, cheap, and convenient in all of our major population centers is critical. Even more critical is to get the people to use it. Again, how do we get the lone commuter driving bumper-to-bumper from suburb to city out of a car and into a mass-transit mode of transportation? A while back, a Department of Energy spokesman said, "What we need are high gasoline prices to reduce consumption." This is a typical bureaucrat's approach. Higher gas prices result in belt tightening somewhere in most budgets and corresponding spending cutbacks.

It's amazing how everyone groused about the high gas prices and the need to address prices early in 2012 when prices approached $4.00 per gallon and the Keystone pipeline was in the headlines. Prices dropped and all discussions stopped. If we don't address the long-term problem regardless of yo-yo gas prices, we'll never become oil independent. The price of gas goes down and it leaves the headlines. It goes up and is the main topic of the country. There are about 250 million vehicles on American roads and that number will certainly rise. Most of them use gasoline. We will be the victims of high gasoline prices until we can get a substantial mix of alternate fuel vehicles on our highways.

Green is good but American is better.

Coal, natural gas, oil, solar, nuclear, wind, and biofuels are either abundant in America or can be developed to reduce our dependence on imported energy. Until now, we haven't had the will to do it and predictably, we have politicized it and ended up with scams like Solyndra.

We shop for goods made in other countries by workers in plants that belch smoke into the environment while regulating our own coal industry to death. We're even building a facility in the Northwest where we will ship our coal to China. Isn't that special? Do we really think that China, where in some cities people on the 10th floor cannot see the street because of the smog, is a better place for our coal to be used than in America? As these countries prosper, their standard of living goes up. They put more cars on the road, increasing the demand for oil and causing us to pay more for a gallon of gas. It's a sort of a boomerang effect caused by the great appetite of the middle class.

We berate oil companies for their large profits and ignore or downplay the fact that they provide many high-paying jobs in America. They're sustainable jobs, not the illusory high-paying green jobs. The only solar panels that we can afford are those made someplace else. Except for Willie Nelson, we laugh at the idea of biofuels.

Maybe we need to turn our regulated head the other way momentarily while we develop our abundant American resources in order to continue our current efforts to become energy independent. By momentarily, I mean five to ten years, which isn't that long considering the task. If it takes that long to reduce America's dependency on foreign energy sources, it'll be time well spent. It just doesn't compute that we import energy from foreign sources that finance terrorism against us and goods from countries that pollute the environment to satisfy our middle class appetite for our too-big-to-succeed retailer's merchandise. We now get most of our energy needs from the U.S. If we could increase that by 20% or 30%, we truly could be energy independent.

We have been hearing T. Boone Pickens proclaim the wonders that converting to natural gas will do for Americans. First, it's American. Second, it's abundant. And most importantly, it will reduce our dependence on foreign oil and the outflow of dollars to countries that, at best, are friendly to us only because we use their oil. Why aren't our legislators and our President out front on this issue? Sure, our President stands in front of a natural gas truck that has been developed and pitches his energy plan. What plan? After the "political moment" has passed, we're still without a defined plan and constant yo yo gas prices.

Supposedly, the U.S. is the number one producer of natural gas. I don't know where the natural gas is, but we should be able to get it to one or more major American cities. What is stopping us from targeting an area, city, or region that is close to natural gas? Find a place with a dense population and a lot of commuters. We could set reasonable goals for the providers and consumers of gasoline to convert to natural gas as a fuel. And, good grief, what's wrong with using the major oil companies that already have a distribution system in their gas stations to establish a network of natural gas stations?

Of course, we'd have to provide incentives to both providers and consumers, but better them than the banks. We have bailed out banks and other institutions that we deemed to be too big to fail with American tax dollars. Why not bail out the average American by reducing his cost of transportation in what is a transportation-intense country?

The cost of building a natural gas distribution network will cost billions of dollars. Americans consume just about 117 billion gallons of gas per year. If we could somehow tap into that number and get $0.50 cents per gallon for building a network, we would have 88 billion dollars to start it. I said "tap," but it would be a tax. As much as it would hurt in the short term, the benefits would make it seem a pittance over the long run.

There are millions of trucks on our highway system that could be converted to natural gas. Instead of waiting for the best-designed natural gas truck, give the major trucking companies an incentive to convert existing trucks to natural gas. I'm sure there's a way to do it, either by mandate or incentives. Major carriers like Fed Ex, UPS, and carriers that support our too-big-to-succeed-retailers consume enormous amounts of diesel fuel. If they could convert to natural gas, our oil consumption would decrease dramatically. We could probably do the same thing with many of the existing cars that Americans drive today. Except for recently, we seldom heard anyone talking about converting passenger cars to natural gas. Why? Evidently, we're better off experimenting with electric cars like the Chevy Volt. How's that working out for us?

What about mandating that within a short period of time, every government vehicle use an alternative American source of energy like natural gas or electricity, or maybe even a hybrid? I can't but believe that government vehicles consume a large amount of gasoline. Certainly, the cost to convert these vehicles and provide facilities for refueling would be expensive, but it would be a commitment to America's energy self-reliance. It would also be a visible reminder to Americans that our government is working for us instead of against us.

Then there's electricity. There's a test going on somewhere in the world with regard to battery exchange stations. When I was running warehouses, we used electric forklifts to retrieve merchandise and move it around the warehouses. When the battery ran down, we took it to a station and exchanged the battery for a fully-charged one. Instead of waiting for someone to invent the battery that's the greatest thing since sliced bread, why can't we design cars that would use existing technology and set up transfer stations that would easily exchange batteries in cars?

Targeting an area like Chicago, we could provide incentives for both providers and consumers to switch to natural gas or electric cars. And again, of course, we already have the infrastructure in place across the country provided by the major oil companies, but we're more comfortable treating oil companies as villains because they're profiting as they bring to us a commodity that we can't do without. Yet, like lemmings, we continue to march to the Apple and Walmart stores and buy products that send our jobs elsewhere!

Given acceptable cars powered by natural gas or batteries as a viable alternative to gasoline, many Americans would switch if there was a dependable supply at reasonably comparable prices. Unfortunately, if we had the availability of natural gas or efficient batteries at reasonable prices, and if there were a meaningful switch causing our consumption of oil to drop, the price of oil and gasoline would probably go down. If that happened, there would be less of an incentive to make the switch. This is the conundrum. Less oil consumption equals less demand equals lower gasoline prices, but if we could wean ourselves from guzzling oil, I believe that America would respond, particularly if the production of alternative fuels resulted in American jobs and we promoted it as a national endeavor.

Andy Leonard

And then there is coal. Oh, no! I understand that we can't believe the hype about "clean coal," but we do have it in abundance. Environmentalists are up in arms over the use of coal, but wouldn't we rather have the regulated use of coal in this country to produce raw materials and electricity than in countries where the regulations are lax or nonexistent?

Since most of our electricity is produced by coal, it would also increase the number of American jobs. Coal, either clean or dirty, is still in great supply in America. More than likely, a coal-fired electric generating plant in America is kinder to the environment than one in China or India. I guess there's a slow transition from coal-fired power plants to the use of natural gas. It looks to me that that is a win-win for American workers. There's an effort to build controversial huge coal exporting facilities in the American Northwest that would ship our coal to Asia. Does it make sense to ship our coal to other countries that would use it to supply electricity to plants that are causing us to lose jobs?

We should be looking at every avenue where we could use coal that is mined in America rather than oil that is pumped from other countries. Certainly, we have to be cautious, but an American job is an American job is an American job. And what's wrong with providing incentives for the American coal industry to engage in research for the more efficient and cleaner use of one of one of our abundant resources that can help reduce our dependence on foreign oil? We have cleaned up our auto emissions and we can probably do it with our coal plants.

We can't blame the person driving on the Kennedy Expressway in Chicago—alone in a gas-guzzling car—

while an elevated train zooms by him as he's stuck in traffic. We can't punish him for living the American dream of a house in the suburbs and a job in the city. We need to make a conscious effort to convince him or her that there's an alternative, and not only and alternative but a less-expensive American job-creating alternative. I believe they'll respond as Americans always have to national crises.

We need to drill, frack, mine, develop, and harvest our natural resources. Again, green is good, but American is better. We sit on our hands and regulate our industries out of existence while other countries exploit our self-guilt. Even though we are becoming more energy independent by the day, we must continue to exploit all our energy sources. As India, China, and emerging economies consume more energy, there will be increased price pressure on all energy sources. It would be an economic boom for America if we were a net supplier rather than a net consumer.

It is unconscionable that boatloads of shipping containers arrive at our shores filled with imported goods and most return to their ports empty. These containers are filled, not just with the stuff we used to make, but they also represent an untold number of lost American jobs.

Ask the employers

It is insane to believe that government monetary policy can create jobs. It is just as insane to keep sending our children to college without the necessary job infrastructure to employ them. Education doesn't create jobs—it enables a person to do a job. Instead of looking to our congressional legion of lawyers, why not turn to the nation's large and mid-sized employers?

It's a lot easier to add new jobs at existing companies with large numbers of employees than to start a new company. Sure, there's a lot of blather about small businesses being the biggest job creators, but it is really difficult to start an innovative new business from scratch. Usually, a small business is created as a result of the synergies created by large companies or the conglomeration of medium to large businesses. Wouldn't it be terrific if we could sit down and determine why American companies are not spending their hoard of cash to create American jobs?

Why is General Electric moving plants and jobs to China? If the answer is purely wages, how do we overcome it? We can't blame General Electric for moving to China to serve the China market but we *can* blame them if five years from now, we are using devices made in China to diagnose American health problems. We need to ask General Electric how they can compete in the world market using American workers. If the answer is wages, where do we need to be? How many high school graduates would be happy working for $10 or $11 an hour? Will these wages put people to work? If not, we're in serious trouble.

Why are most of the Apple devices made someplace else? Is the answer purely wages? Sooner or later, we are going to have to face the fact that the markets of China, India, and many other economic regions dwarf the American market. It will take a couple of generations before they catch up to us in the area of wages. In the meantime, we are sending our children to college to do what?

Tax the Internet

There was an Internet sales tax bill looming in Congress. Great! Shopping on the Internet has gone

THE MIDDLE CLASS FEEDS UPON ITSELF

from being a minuscule to a major sales factor for retailers. It is rare to find someone who has not bought a product on the Internet. In our "I, me, me" society, price and selection have switched many of us from shopping locally to shopping on the Internet. A friend purchased the latest, greatest LED television from a company in New York and saved over $240 in sales tax by buying it online. And not only the taxes, but also the purchase price was lower than local retailers and the shipping was free. Even if the electronic giant Best Buy could match that deal, they would have charged Florida sales tax. *Mea culpa, mea culpa, mea maxima culpa!*

So instead of helping a local retailer keep a local person employed, he took the least expensive route. Can you blame him? I recently bought a safe from Amazon for our American Legion post. When I asked the woman at the other end of the line who, by the way, was in South Dakota—if she needed our tax-exempt certificate, she replied that they didn't collect sales tax from Florida purchasers.

The argument is that it would be too costly for Internet retailers to maintain the tax base structure of every state and municipality into which they ship merchandise. In today's world, a high school senior could do it. The solution is easy. Tax any Internet retailer at the highest sales tax rate of any state or municipality and send the tax dollars to where the recipient's sales tax would be collected. So tax Internet sales at 9% and call it a sales/jobs tax. It is patently unfair to allow Internet retailers not to collect and pay a sales tax to the purchaser's taxing authority. Again, in the "I, me, me" environment, many Internet sales go untaxed and destroy local job opportunities. It was dis heartening to hear Sean Hannity rail against the recent Internet sales tax bill on FOX. He and other anti-tax do-dos make no connection with the uncollected sales tax and local jobs. As I have said earlier, not only do they avoid sales taxes but they do not have the overhead costs involved with setting up retail locations.

Last year, there was a report that there were over 100 billion downloads from Apple and Google. If half of them were from the United States and they sold for a dollar each and were taxed at a 9% sales tax rate, we could have collected over 4.5 billion dollars in sales taxes! Christmas 2013 was an example of how pervasive Internet shopping has become. Consumers who had to live with late Christmas deliveries berated both UPS and FedEx. Consumes waiting for last-minute deals were expecting to get their shipments on time for Christmas with a very short delivery window. I had no sympathy.

Focus on your local economy and government.

It's time we quit following the trends that kill the jobs around us and focus on what's good for the space we live in, whether it's a small town or a neighborhood in a big city. An easy but time-consuming step would be to bank locally. It was awfully hard to change our bank accounts from my regional mega bank to our local community bank. Everything was on auto deposit and it was a chore to get the Social Security Administration, my pension provider, and others to make the switch, but once it was done, the money stayed—and is put to use—in the community. Why should I put my money in an entity that more than likely has little effect on our local economy?

How about eating at local restaurants? I generally

THE MIDDLE CLASS FEEDS UPON ITSELF

avoid eating at national chain eateries, but I have to be honest and say that we don't have many national chains where I live. There are many within a short drive, but we choose to patronize local businesses whenever possible. It may even be a way for the middle class to get back at the 2% by reducing the sales of McDonald's and the like and driving the stock price down. I dread the day when an Applebee or Outback opens in our area, as it will undoubtedly hurt our locally-owned restaurants.

Unfortunately, very few local retail businesses can survive in the face of Walmart, Home Depot, Lowe's, and other mega-retailers. They could survive with our support. Look at all of the vacant retail space in shopping centers and strip malls across the country. And even if you must shop at the mega-chains, don't use the automatic checkout lines. Our local Home Depot usually has only one live checkout person. Most shoppers, including those ex-union members, opt to check out their own merchandise, thus depriving someone of a job. The argument is that, like part-time employees, self-checkout reduces employee costs and results in lower prices. I guess price is everything.

Do your shopping locally for drugs and sundries. Not all insurance plans make it easy, but if you can afford it, give the local pharmacist your business. Complain to your insurer that you would like your money kept in the local economy. Complain to your representatives in Congress that the Walmarts, Walgreens, and CVSs shouldn't have an unfair advantage over the local pharmacy. It probably won't do much good, but it'll make you feel a lot better.

Get involved with local government. Most of our legion of lawyers cut their spending teeth at the local or state level. They stick around for two or three terms or more, spend our tax dollars, and then leave without recourse. They cater to local special interests to get elected and re-elected with little concern for the ongoing burden on taxpayers they leave in their wake. How many cities are facing huge pension and healthcare bills that are the result of long gone politicians catering to the block voting of teachers and public employees?

The only way to stop it is to go to council or commission meetings and question every dollar spent. Write state legislators and question every dollar spent. The best cure for government gone wild is to vote against unnecessary tax dollars spent for political purposes. Many local and state governments have taken on the budget-breaking obligations of future benefits to government employees, public safety workers, and teachers. A good many of the obligations were negotiated or enacted by politicians who have gone to greener political pastures. As they advance to other layers of government, the stakes get bigger, elections get more expensive, and the need to cater to special-interest groups increases. Instead of being ignored, we need to create a special-interest group called the taxpayer.

Create your own term limits. When politics becomes a career, we approve and perpetuate an elite-governing class that, by necessity, becomes detached from the average American. You can't continually get re-elected to an office or move up in the system without catering to one special-interest group or another. The simple answer is to not re-elect incumbent candidates for more than the number of terms that you are comfortable with regardless of their party affiliation. A long-term politician becomes an expert at politics with no guarantee that he or she is an expert at governing. What they become good at is mucking up and complicating the system to the point that the average taxpayer doesn't understand it. They create a system that relies on career self-serving bureaucrats to function.

Become a member of the independent party. Abandon your party affiliation and let the politicians win your vote. Our area Florida is predominantly Republican. It's too easy for politicians to register Republican and believe they automatically have won a block of votes. What if we all registered as independents, requiring them to win our vote? It isn't easy to do this with our primary system if you want to actively be involved with choosing the candidates of your party, whether they be Republicans or Democrats. It would be much easier if we had an open primary system.

Fix our Job infrastructure

We need to work on the American job infrastructure. Somehow, we have to figure out how to get the things we use every day back to being made in America. How can Walmart get that shirt on the counter for $4.99 or $5.99 all the way from China? Is it just the wages or is it a combination of the wage differential, federal, state and local government regulations, the price of transportation and other costs, and the sheer size and efficiency of Walmart's logistic system? It could be argued that Walmart's logistic system creates what is close to a monopoly when it comes to retailing.

The average unemployment check in America is about $290.00 per week. What if, after a reasonable length of job search time, instead of sending an unemployment check, we sent a voucher for the $290.00 to the unemployed worker? He or she could then go to a company that could use the voucher as an incentive from the government to hire the person on a trial basis into a higher-paying job that needs to be filled.

Once the employee demonstrates the ability to do the job, the vouchers would stop. The vouchers could be used by a company to start an enterprise that would bring back some of the jobs we've lost to lower-paying countries. It couldn't last forever, but if it takes $11.00 per hour to make widgets competitively, the $290.00 would contribute $7.25 to the $11.00 and give the company some breathing room to get the business going and the unemployed worker still gets the money in a paycheck. We could probably do the same thing with some of our "entitlement" payments, too.

It may be that we need to change our attitude about the obligations an employer has to its employees other than providing a job. We need to look at manufacturing and the start-up costs that manufacturers would incur reviving American production of the items we use. You can't get your arms around the number of jobs that we have lost in manufacturing the stuff we use every day. I do believe that for every ten to twenty manufacturing jobs in America, there's a trickle-up multiplier in the neighborhood of three or four to determine the net jobs created. It's distressing to note that in the near future, the majority of private sector jobs created in America will be in the service sector—restaurant servers, hairdressers, and cooks instead of machinists, engineers, and warehouse workers.

THE MIDDLE CLASS FEEDS UPON ITSELF

It's true that manufacturing the stuff we use every day won't include many high-tech or green jobs, but so what? We continue to need consumable products. Fans, tape rules, hammers, light bulbs, and clothes are like toothpaste, trash bags, and razorblades—we use them up, wear them out, lose them, and buy more of them. We need to make them in America with American workers. The result will be a ripple-up effect and some high-paying jobs will follow.

We may need a reset. With the minimum wage over $7.00 per hour and the real prospect of it going up to $10.00, how can we compete with the India and Chinas of the world? What happens if Africa or other countries becomes low-wage players in production? Without a huge base of American workers making what we use every day and spending their money locally, we are in serious trouble. All the talk about green jobs, high-paying tech jobs, and government-sponsored infrastructure jobs is just that—talk! We're in an international, very competitive marketplace. The question is, will we adapt or continue on the road that keeps us from being competitive with other nations?

Although you don't hear much about it, part of the solution to the government rescuing General Motors was to reset and reduce wages and benefits. We may have to do the same in other industries in order to get the jobs back. A thriving manufacturing sector and a resurgence of local retail businesses would result in millions of American jobs. Don't ask the politicians for help. Most of them need the union-voting blocks for re-election.

Making the stuff in America that we use every day, from toothpicks to tractors, isn't a glamorous endeavor. The blue-collar jobs required aren't especially attractive to the connected high-tech youth of today. You don't hear about many parents who want their kids to work on an assembly line, in a warehouse, or in the associated low-tech jobs. If we made the stuff we use every day in America, there would be millions of those jobs. If we can't or won't fill them with our current work force, it may be a way to solve the immigration problem. Oops!

There is a video floating around the Internet that says that if we increase our purchase of American-made products by only 5%, we would create millions of jobs? The problem is finding those products. The solution is to make them here.

The Federal Trade Commission regulates mergers and acquisitions. The following is from their web page:

The Bureau of Competition is committed to preventing mergers and acquisitions that are likely to reduce competition and lead to higher prices, lower quality goods or services, or less innovation.

What about jobs? In their pursuit of maximizing profits, companies buy, sell, and merge with other companies. Almost every merger or acquisition results in consolidation of operations that eliminates jobs and that in some cases, reduces wages. The FTC doesn't spend much time investigating small businesses. Rather; it focuses on big business with many employees. High on the list of the FTC's examination process should be an evaluation of the impact on American jobs.

Restore loyalty and get a conscience

Americans have lost what used to be strong ties to their life interests. Union members lose their comradeship with one another. Catholics lose their deference to papal dictum. Some Baptists vote with color rather than church teachings. No longer does salvation trump all else. We vote on social issues that conflict with our religious beliefs as if a trip to the confessional makes it okay. Women could be seen cheering Bill Clinton at the last Democratic Convention—and they weren't all blondes. He is someone who brought disgrace to the presidency and demeaned women in the process.

This from a June 2008 issue of *Newsweek:*

http://www.thedailybeast.com/newsweek/ 2008/06/22/believers-in-the-pews-and-the- polling-booth.html

Still, black Protestants remain loyal Democrats, regardless of how important religion is to an individual's life--77 percent of black Protestants said they vote Democratic, whether they attended weekly services or not. Prominent intellectual and activist Cornel West points out that this is largely due to the black community's historic ties to the Democratic Party, specifically during the civil-rights movement. "It's a matter of principle," West says. "Not just a matter of partisanship." This staunch support exists despite some black churches' conservative views on social issues like abortion and same-sex marriage. While the survey finds that those with high levels of religious commitment tend to oppose abortion and public acceptance of homosexuality, black Protestants remain steadfast Democratic voters. West and others believe that this is because for members of black churches and of the black community in general, "issues of economic and social justice tend to supersede issues of abortion and same sex-marriage."

Andy Leonard

*In other words, issues of equality and civil-rights
continue to override any moral qualms black Christian
voters may have with Democratic politics. That can
only be good news for Barack Obama, a churchgoing
black Protestant himself*

In light of the above, it's interesting that in May of
2013, the Illinois State Legislature failed to consider a
bill that would legalize same-sex marriage. President
Obama went to Illinois to endorse the issue, but
Catholic and African-American church leaders were
strongly opposed to the measure and it never came to
the floor. It's easy to assume that many of the church
members voted for the President. Salvation must be
coming back. The bill finally passed, but it was
interesting to see the early blowback by the church
leaders.

Issues of responsible governance are ignored. It's
clear that in 2012, we voted the person into the White
House with the least ability to solve our job crises. No
wonder that one of Hillary Clinton's first announcement
in 2013 as a possible candidate in 2016 was a
statement supporting the lesbian-gay-bisexual-
transgender cause. Let's not even think about electing
another ageing lawyer as president—even if it's a
woman—to the job that needs someone with an
agenda focused on our economic issues rather than
one who panders to minority and social interests.

I believe that, in a frenzy of conscience, we
elected our first black president and suffered for it with
one of the worst presidencies in recent history. Let's
not make the same mistake with a woman. We don't
need another frenzy of conscience just to check off the
box on some sort of national bucket list that says we
have elected a female president.

THE MIDDLE CLASS FEEDS UPON ITSELF

There are 317 million Americans. Why should we settle for another Clinton or for that matter another Bush. There're too many other qualified women and men who could assume the presidency. A royal family we do not need. We need to let common sense prevail. Politicians like Hillary Clinton too often deflect from critical issues and instead pander to voters and are defined by their stand on controversial issues such as abortion, contraception, evolution, and LBGT causes, including same sex marriage. Issues that are better resolved between and individuals and their personal moral code.

We seem to have ignored the fact that we all have the right to exercise our free will on these moral issues. Regardless of a person's flavor of religion, these issues should be left to a person's relationship with their God if any. On these issues, a person should be allowed to act based upon their personal set of beliefs. We should be guided by our own moral compass rather than have someone else's set of beliefs written into law. Write the laws to allow free-will choices on all issues and get over it. The religious right appears to have little faith in the strength of their brethren's faith.

When I was running a distribution center for True Value, I would go to the local Walmart on weekends and would watch some of our union employees—the same ones who were beating us up over wages and benefits—pushing cartloads of non-union made merchandise to their cars. At the same time, union leaders were spending money on ads with workers singing, "Look for the union label." The same merchandise was available at the True Value stores that would give them a 10% discount but instead, there they were, shopping at the company that was putting True Value stores out of business. Not only were they disloyal to the company that employed them but they were also disloyal to the union that represented them. Once again, price trumped loyalty.

I bridled at the fact that teachers who were members of one of the biggest public employee union in the country would ask parents to shop for back-to-school supplies at an office supply company with no union employees. Of course, the company was giving a small rebate to the school districts.

Even today, at Walmart stores around the country, former members of some of the largest unions walk the aisles of Walmart looking for bargains. Even more ironic, some of them work part-time at one of the most notorious anti-union companies on earth. It's amusing to see a bumper sticker in a Walmart parking lot that extols the fact the owner drives only American cars while pushing a cartload of foreign-made merchandise to their American car. What about walking in American shoes? Most of them don't know that some retailers still employ union labor and most of them don't care. Again, it is the "I, I, me, me" society we live in.

If you don't agree with liberal MSNBC, drop Comcast Cable, their parent company, and don't watch any of their other cable channels. If you don't agree with FOX's conservative leaning, boycott and unsubscribe to any News Corp properties. And when you do, tell them the reason you are taking the action. These two giant too-big-to-succeed entities foist their political views on us with little recourse. We can fight back with our wallets.

The collapse of a textile plant in Bangladesh made news worldwide. It was a tragedy resulting in the deaths of over 600 workers and the natural knee-jerk reaction was to blame the owners of the factory. They should, and most likely will, be held responsible. Unfortunately, in low-wage areas of the world where there's cutthroat competition for contracts to produce goods for our major retailers, worker safety isn't a prerequisite for success. In many cases, it has been reported that when workers are asked if they would rather see safety improved or an increase in wages, they opt for increased wages.

It's an ugly and unfortunate conundrum. If the supplier does both, it becomes uncompetitive. The least costly alternative is to raise wages slightly to keep workers happy. The probable reality is that the workers weren't forced to work in the building and in many cases, the companies that ordered the goods didn't know or care about the dangerous conditions. Regardless, the driver is a manufacturer's fragile connection with retailers throughout the world and the retailer's constant pressure to lower the cost of goods.

How many of us after the Bangladesh tragedy made the decision not to buy products made in Bangladesh or made the effort to find out what retailers were placing orders for the finished goods? And if we did and decided to boycott the culprits, how will it affect the lives of the Bangladeshi workers? I suspect that most of us offered casual sympathy but did nothing else. In most cases, price trumps conscience.

Focus on the Region

Ours is a large and diverse country. New York is different than Philadelphia. Chicago is different than Kansas City. Dallas is different than LA. Portland is different than Denver. We speak the same language but have broad regional differences in our lifestyles and in our local economies. There's no single solution for creating jobs in these diverse areas. There must be a way to set up regional enterprise zones that could develop bottom-up solutions for creating jobs rather than the top-down solutions that our politicians and bureaucrats put forth.

Florida and Ohio's rejection of the bullet train is a great example of politicians and bureaucrats gone wild. If not for common sense prevailing over political pandering, we would have two empty bullet trains. One would be going from Orlando to Tampa and back and one would be going from Cleveland to Columbus and back. It would cost the American taxpayers billions, but Rachel Maddow would be happy.

Let's divide the country into logical economic regions and get the best CEOs, entrepreneurs, financiers, and other non-government people involved with economic planning. They are the ones with real-life experience in creating and sustaining private sector jobs. They are the ones who could do it, not Barack Obama, George W. Bush, Nancy Pelosi, or John Boehner. I would—grudgingly of course—include local union leaders where necessary. Unfortunately, it would certainly be mucked up because our politicians and bureaucrats wouldn't let it happen without their participation.

Florida and its adjacent states rely on tourism and retirees. No matter how hard they try, Florida politicians will never make it an industrial hub. Forget about bullet trains and focus on tourism, leisure, retirees, medical services, and agriculture. If federal money is to be spent in Florida, it should be in these five critical areas. Spend money on enticing the national and international tourist to visit Florida. Spend it on beaches, boat ramps, bike routes, golf courses, and other amenities that make Florida an international tourist and retirement destination and create jobs.

The business of agriculture, both land based and aquatic, should be nurtured. We are eating fish from the Mekong River instead of locally-raised fish. This should leave a bad taste in your mouth. The local Florida Walmart sells oranges from California—sort of like Chinese mushrooms. I have no experience in agriculture but can't help thinking that Florida and adjacent states can supply increased quantities of fruit, vegetables, and seafood to the world.

If the American people were given the chance to see such a regional process developed to create jobs in their area with government cooperation rather than restrictions and intervention, they might have a different perspective on the value of our elected leaders and the political process.

Get serious about downsizing government.

Maybe downsizing is not the correct word. Streamlining probably is a better choice. It has nothing to do with big government vs. small government. It has to do with efficient government. The Defense Department would be a good model. Do we really need an Army, Air Force, Navy, Marine Corps, and Coast Guard and all their separate command-and-control functions, weapon systems and procurement departments? Do we need an Army Reserve and the National Guard?

The Congressional hearings on sexual harassment in the military gave us a good visual. Twelve decorated military high-ranking officers sat side-by-side in front of the committee. Each of them could be thought of as the pinnacle of a pyramid with thousands of men and women below them. It isn't hard to imagine that there's considerable overlap and redundancies in the functions beneath and above them.

Isn't there even a small possibility that we can consolidate bases across the US and other countries? The Armed Forces History Museum website lists the top ten elite military units. That includes the Seals, Delta Force, and other "elite" units. You would think it might be possible to consolidate them into one cross-trained force. I am a veteran and have many friends who served in the various branches of the service. Many of them have extreme loyalty to their branch of the service and in many cases, to their specialty such as the paratroopers, but their service was in a different time. Today's all-volunteer and highly-technical fighting force has changed drastically. Rather than weakening it, streamlining it would probably strengthen it and reduce the burden on taxpayers.

The Pentagon is shrouded with an impenetrable cloak. Their budgets are cloudy and in some cases, incomprehensible. It's increasingly important for the United States to have the strongest most efficient military on the planet, but we need a modern military structure that eliminates waste—and in some cases, fraud—in order to effectively and efficiently use taxpayer dollars.

Instead of just reducing the number men in the Army and Marines as is the current plan offered by our President and Defense Secretary Leon Panetta, streamline and strengthen the military from top to bottom. Start with our military and move on to other government departments. A win-win for the American

THE MIDDLE CLASS FEEDS UPON ITSELF

taxpayer.

Our legion of lawyers has made governing so complicated that the process has become more important than results. Entrenched bureaucrats, experts in the application of laws, codes, and ordinances, control our lives. Instead of facilitating commerce, they hinder it, throwing up regulatory roadblocks in the interest of self-preservation. Big Brother has the power.

Operating efficiently and effectively should be the goal of all government offices. Most Americans on the outside looking in would probably agree with that. Unfortunately, like the Pentagon, job preservation, expanded spheres of influence, and career path become the goals for bureaucrats and once created, there's no way to measure or manage most government agencies and the services they provide. When a business doesn't run efficiently and effectively, it fails. Our government is on a course to failure in that regard. Rather than figure out a solution to the looming crisis that may cripple us, our leaders have again taken their heads out of the sand and decided to tax us some more.

To be redundant, if you can't measure it, you can't manage it. Any successful businessperson knows it. Any family with a decent credit rating knows it. It's one of the primary rules of effective management that both politicians and voters seem to ignore. We have no reasonable way to measure the effectiveness of local, state, or federal government. Sure, most municipalities and states balance their budget and everybody has a plan to balance our federal budget. The balanced budget doesn't address whether or not government is efficient. All it means is that we have enough revenue to cover our expenses, but it doesn't answer the question: are we spending tax dollars efficiently?

Every law, bill, ordinance, and statute complicates the life of some taxpayer. Every one of them should have an expiration date that would force a serious review of the intended and unintended consequences. We will continue to expand government until we develop an unbiased non-political way to measure the efficiency of government, whether local, state or federal. It is a Herculean task, but so was putting a man on the moon. The Internal Revenue Service, National Security Administration, and General Services Administration scandals should scare the hell out of all of us. The entrenched bureaucrats in these government departments are perfect examples of government gone wild. Whether you call it bureaucracy creep or government extrapolated, we need to rein it in.

I will wait silently, like many Americans, for the time when government-gone-wild is tamed, for the time when government works for the people, for the time when our leaders lead us, for the time when we quit pitting one class of Americans against another and when the middle class, regains prosperity. The long wait, unfortunately, will probably include choking on the occasional pizza topped with the dreaded Chinese mushrooms.

ABOUT THE AUTHOR

Andy lives with his wife Donna in southwest Florida. The Middle Class Feeds Upon Itself is his personal commentary concerning the troubled middle class in America.

Andy Leonard

www.ingramcontent.com/pod-product-compliance
Lightning Source LLC
Chambersburg PA
CBHW050126280326
41933CB00010B/1259